Endorsements

God desires to show Himself strong in the earth but He needs people who are willing to totally submit to Him with all of their hearts and by faith, declare and decree His word out of their mouths over their lives and the lives of those they love. Through the power of God's Word and prayer, what the devil meant for evil, was totally turned around for good. Confess the Word of God over your life and your loved ones and watch the same power that worked for Tina work for you.

While reading this book my faith was increased, tears of joy poured down my face, and hope filled my heart! I hope that women and men will read this book and know that the power of God is bigger than any mountain and can heal everyone! Yes, the power of God is on display in *I Need a Day to Pray* and it brings about everlasting change!

CeCe Winans-Love
Co-pastor with her husband, Alvin,
Nashville Life Church, Nashville, TN
Multiple Grammy Awarded Gospel Artist

Tina has taken her life's experiences and put them to practical prayers, affirmations, declarations and proclamations that will bless the life of all who read this! I will decree these benedictions over my entire life and family! POWERFUL!

Donnie McClurkin
Pastor of Perfecting Faith Church, Freeport, NY
Multiple Grammy Awarded Gospel Artist

If you want to see things in your life change, then this book is for you. *I Need a Day to Pray* is a true testament of Tina Campbell's faith and a transparent message of how one can turn pain, challenges, and despair into triumph. This book will help guide you daily in your prayer life, offering practical life lessons, prayers and declarations supported by God's Word. It is evident that Tina has reclaimed her rightful place and she is ready to soar. Through effectual prayer, wisdom redeems time and makes the most out of life's setbacks and creates greater opportunities.

Bishop Paul S. and Dr. Debra B. Morton
Co-Founders of the Full Gospel Baptist Church Fellowship
Pastors of Changing a Generation
Full Gospel Baptist Church, Atlanta, GA
Greater St. Stephen Full Gospel Baptist Church,
New Orleans, LA

Over thirty five years ago we experienced betrayal, hurt, and disappointments as a result of a serious church fight. It was so tragic we were both holding on to past hurts, unforgiveness, and the betrayal we experienced from others. God clearly showed us He could not use our lives if we would not let go of those past hurts. God lead us to Hebrews 9:14 and we daily confessed that 'the blood of Jesus cleanses our conscious of dead works.'

Although the memory of the incidents didn't leave, the pain associated with the incident left.

In our first conversation with Tina after her ordeal, we told her about the power of the blood of Jesus and that, through her daily confession, the pain of the situation would eventually leave. This book reveals that Tina heeded our counsel and is winning through her confession and the power of the blood of Jesus.

We recommend every person who has ever been hurt, betrayed, lied to, lied on, or abused apply the principles Tina outlines in this book. Your life will be accelerated to freedom!

Bishop I. V. and Pastor Bridget Hilliard,
Founders of New Light Church Austin,
Beaumont, and Houston, TX

Tina has a testimony that should be told on the mountain top. Though the circumstances that brought her to write this book were very specific, the words that came from her heart are tailor-made for every believer. The anointing of God permeates a room when these confessions are made. They are personal and powerful in nature. The Word of the Lord declares that with our heart we believe unto righteousness, but with our mouth confession is made unto salvation. Those who read the words of this book with a right spirit and clean heart will be saved, delivered, and experience victorious living in Christ Jesus.

I believe that 'what could kill a person' will be the same thing that will 'make them strong' when they are delivered from it. Tina received strength through these prayers and confessions during a very difficult time in her life. I touch and agree with her that the readers of this book will receive double strength and mega deliverance. There is life and death in the power of the tongue. These words speak life and, as people read them, they will live and not die! They will READ, RECEIVE, REPEAT and be REVIVED.

Thank you, Tina, for sharing the most intimate details of your deliverance. The enemy of life is defeated by the Blood of the Lamb and the word of your testimony. Because you have told it (and shared) your victory over it ... many people will obtain victory and overcome. Selah.

Apostle Kimberly Daniels
Author, Founder and Pastor of Spoken Word Ministries,
Jacksonville, FL

I Need A Day To Pray

I Need A Day To Pray

Tina Campbell

GEE TREE
CREATIVE

WOODLAND HILLS, CALIFORNIA

I Need a Day to Pray

Published by:
Gee Tree Creative
21700 Oxnard Street, Suite 2030
Woodland Hills, CA 91367
www.IamTinaCampbell.com

Tina Campbell, Publisher
Dr. Tandie Mazule and Dr. Evon Peet, Editors
Yvonne Rose/Quality Press.info, Production Coordinator
Printed Page, Interior Format
Donnell Bryant, Cover Designer

Unless otherwise noted, Scripture quotations are from the King James Version of the Bible (Public Domain: www.biblegateway.com).

Dedication

To my lion heart daddy who is in heaven now. You showed me how to pray earnestly, specifically, and according to the Word. You showed me the discipline of fasting and praying. I'll always remember the intense prayers as you prayed in the Spirit for us and read Bible stories to us around the bed as kids. Daddy, I also watched you pray for people and, through God's authority, you'd help facilitate their deliverance in church services or while you were evangelizing at parks or jails. You would stand in God's authority and command the devil to shut up and leave, and he would. I had to do the same thing to get from where I was to where I am and it was a challenge, but I had the example of what to do based on what you taught me and based on watching you do it. Daddy, you were a general in God's army. You passed the baton off to me and now I'm running with it.

To my mommy, who listened to Bible tapes all day and night, every day and night of my life except Sunday, when we were at church all day. You showed me what "keeping your mind stayed on Jesus" actually looked like. You prayed for us every night of my life so I always woke up with blessed oil in the center of my head. You literally tried to carry my sorrow and pain for me during this process. Only God could succeed at that, but you certainly tried. You are the embodiment of God's love and mercy. Everyone who meets you is better off because of it. Anybody can follow you to get to Jesus. I love you with my whole heart and I'm proud that you are MY mommy.

Dad and Mom, you laid a proper foundation. You lived for Christ and lead me to Him. I'll always be grateful for my magnificent parents.

Special Thanks

To my husband, my best friend, my strong, courageous, beautiful love of my life, Teddy Campbell. We prayed this prayer every week for over a year and submitted to its truths; now look at what God has done. I watched you transform into the true priest of our home and I'm just blown away by God's love and truth and power manifested in your life. NOBODY IS GREATER THAN OUR GOD!!! I'm honored to follow you and I'm looking forward to loving you forever.

To my amazing, beautiful, loving children. You all are a great source of inspiration and strength for Mommy. We became stronger believers as we watched God hold our family together and make us better. My babies got to see with their own eyes that God loves us, He can do anything, and He never fails. Mommy loves you but y'all know Jesus loves you more.

To all my sisters and brothers. You all stood with me and prayed for me without ceasing and without judgment. I mean, Lisa and Shanta, you started our family prayer line twice a day. All of y'all called or came by or kept my kids or just listened or spoke words of encouragement to me. Sometimes, just like Mama, you tried to carry my pain for me. You all told me you were in it with me until I came out and you all kept your word. I love y'all Atkins (including my in-law bros and sis) with all the love that I have inside of me.

Alvin and CeCe (Winans) Love, what can I say about you two? You ushered me into spiritual warfare; you showed me what peace and harmony in a marriage, home, and church looked like. You prayed with me, for me, you rebuked me when I needed it. You gave me the truth with love. You introduced me to the Towles. THANK YOU.

Elder Barry and Kathy Towles, only God in heaven could love me and Teddy enough to hook us up with the two of you. After being prayed over and prophesied to by you, I was definitively sure that you both were on assignment from Heaven concerning me and Teddy. You both helped cultivate what God placed in my husband and me. You pushed us to walk in the authority God has given us. You both saw in us what we didn't yet see or trust in ourselves, and you pulled it out of us before we could even say no. We'll love and appreciate you forever.

Tim Carmon, thanks for being an honest and bold friend. Thanks for rebuking both me and Teddy according to God's Word and not accepting our arguments of self-pity or our decisions to quit. Thanks for being consistent and being there whenever we needed it. Love you.

Apostle Kim Daniels, thank you for praying with me any time of the day and night. Thanks for giving me knowledge and understanding of spiritual matters and instructing me in spiritual warfare. You're an awesome teacher and friend.

Aunto and Uncle Warryn, thanks for helping us keep it together in every way that y'all could. Thanks for loving both of us and understanding even when it was challenging to keep hanging in there with us.

The G's, I appreciate y'all for all the love and support. Thanks for just letting me be me through bad and worst and good and better. I love y'all.

Pastor Mel and Desiree Ayers, for one of the greatest, most Jesus filled, sound doctrine teaching churches on this side of heaven, In His Presence Church. You directed us to God weekly and we thank you, Pastor Charles and Teresa Lollis, (Uncle Charles and Aunt Teresa). Y'all are just the best there ever was. I got my foundation in the gospel right at Evangelistic COGIC and y'all laid it well. I love y'all to life.

Dennis and Gladys Dodsend, thanks for your constant prayers and encouragement.

To all of my extended family, friends, supporters, and everyone who prayed for me, my husband and my children, individually or collectively, as we fought for our family's miracle, you have a HUGE place in my heart. I pray that the blessings of the Lord overtake you, suddenly, and make your life a greater testimony, all for the glory of our awesome God.

Donnell Bryant, you came on board with great ideas and designs; a great commitment of your time and considerable patience. Your art work is supreme and I thank you for designing this and everything else I'm doing.

Pastor Donnie McClurkin, Bishop I.V. and Dr. Bridgette Hilliard, Bishop Paul and Dr. Debra Morton, and Bishop Paul Adefarisin, thank you for your prayers, support, wisdom, and kind words. You are all invaluable to me and to the whole body of Christ.

To my lawyer Darrell Miller. If you had not told me that this journal to God was a book, I'm not so sure I would ever have shared it with the world. Thank you for encouraging me and investing so much of your time and insight. You've been much more than a lawyer throughout this process. You've been a trusted confidant and a dear friend. Thank you for caring and thank you for your great wisdom and overall assistance with all of this. I appreciate you.

Dr. Clarice, you brought your God sense, wisdom, and kindness to this project with your amazing foreword. I appreciate you. And thank you for your new book *Ridiculous Miracles*. It gave me great encouragement late one night while trying to manage the process of independently releasing this work.

To my amazing editors Dr. Tandie Mazule and Dr. Evon Peet. After our first meeting over the phone, I knew you two were Godsends. Our call felt more like a developing friendship rather than professional partnership. I just knew that this relationship would extend into my future. Thank you for your insight, prayers, prophesies, sweet spirits, excellence, and overall commitment to this project.

To my book packager and production coordinator Yvonne Rose of Quality Press, who worked diligently to complete the final steps to publish my book, Thank you for being there at the right time.

Table of Contents

I Need a Day to Pray

Foreword

When you have the opportunity and feel compelled to read a book even before you pick it up, and then find yourself totally and completely immersed, saturated, and soaked in its rich and defining journey; then this is the book that will hold you from the first syllable on the first page to the last period of the last sentence. This book has been crafted by the inspiration of the Spirit of God. It has a life of its own, has traveled and traversed the crisscrossing paths of a life in turmoil, been taken to the outer limits of a life out of control, and then miraculously brought back into a trajectory marked by purpose, direction, love, and the desire to share the magnificent outcome with the world.

Nothing about this book is left to the imagination. Tina has mastered the essence of life itself without really intending to and uses this book to take you, just as it did her, on the journey of a lifetime. She finds herself engulfed in wisdom she never knew she had, insight she never dreamed of acquiring, a destiny she didn't know existed, and a legacy she fought to conquer and bequeath to everyone who reads her story. This book, every single page of it, is intentional in its design, strategic in its direction, and irresistible in its message and mission.

Tina would say, don't follow me, follow Jesus; but in reading her story, you cannot help but live her life with her, become transfixed and transformed and, if you're willing, end up changed in countenance, conduct, and character. It's a journey worth taking!

Dr. Clarice Fluitt
Strategic Consultant, Personal Advisor, Motivational Speaker
Author and Founder Clarice Fluitt Ministries

Introduction

My life looked pretty good on the outside. I'm a preacher's kid who was basically born and raised in church. I came to know God as a kid, got serious about Him as a teen, then changed my mind and strayed, but came back to Him as a young adult. I loved the Lord and chose to have a relationship with Him but I struggled, for many years, to have a committed walk.

My church attendance and participation in the choir was consistent but my prayer time, worship time, Bible reading time, and overall communication with God was totally inconsistent. That remained the case, even after becoming an accomplished gospel music artist, wife, and mother of five children. I didn't practice sin, but I also didn't necessarily practice holy living; I just kind of did what was convenient and customary for me to do. For all intents and purposes, let's just be honest and say, I held to my religious practices.

Now, if I had an abundance of free time, I'd pray, read my Bible, and spend time with God. But, if that time and space did not present itself in my hectic schedule, I'd basically get my whole Godly experience at church, in a quick prayer before going on stage, or while being on stage singing gospel music. I would not return to it until I came back to church or to my next concert.

Oh, and then there was the quick bedtime prayer that was more of a tradition than a passion. I'd pray a routine prayer, more from my head than from my heart, just before falling to sleep. Truth is, there was no constant communion or committed relationship with me and God. He was not always scheduled into my daily agendas. I didn't talk to Him regularly and He didn't talk to me regularly, but I considered myself to be a believer and follower of Christ. I never could seem to overcome my challenges of anger, rage, unforgiveness, complaining, selfishness, anxiety, distrust, constant irritability, lack of temperance, need to control everything, pride, and the list goes on, because I didn't have a discipline of consistently seeking God in prayer, studying the Bible, believing all of it, and walking in it.

I simply didn't have an existence that was indicative of an exclusive adherence to many of the Biblical truths that should have governed my life, because I didn't actually adhere to many of those truths; some of them, but not all of them; much of the time, but not all of the time. My faith was massive in theory but small in the face of challenges. My joy was situational. My peace was rare, and I maintained a stressed, frustrated, discontented life while professing to be who I really wanted to be and thought I was, but actually only was in theory. I did love God and I believed a more fulfilled, overcoming Christian life was possible, but my relationship with God was never prioritized like other things in my life were, so I never actually learned how to properly activate my faith, receive God's grace, and live as the Bible said I could.

I got tired and decided that in 2013 I would make a concentrated effort to acquaint myself with my Savior Jesus, know Him like I never had before, and be transformed by Him like I knew I could have and should have already been. I wrote out a prayer, confession, and declaration based on the knowledge I had of the Bible and intended to pray, confess, and believe on God's Word until I saw victory manifest in my natural life. I started a 40 day fast and began finding my way back to Jesus.

It seems like as soon as I made the decision to have a serious relationship with Jesus, all hell broke loose in my life. I became aware of my husband's countless years and scenarios of infidelity, my father got cancer and died in two and a half months, I had loads of professional problems, I had financial challenges, and the list goes on. My youngest baby, who initially slept through the night, began waking all through the night once the hardships began, so I maintained a restless state of existence. I struggled with depression, anxiety, suicidal thoughts, and even attempted suicide. I was enraged and at times violent. I struggled with thoughts and plans of having some of the people murdered who hurt me.

Fortunately, I never carried out any of those plans, but still I contemplated it, deeply, because I was as low and heavy in spirit as one could be. I wanted to hurt people because I was a hurting person. It's like the words to the Mary Mary song "Shackles," "everything that could go wrong/all went wrong at one time/some much pressure fell on me/I thought I was gone lose my mind."

My whole initial decision to get my life in line with Jesus was greatly challenged and I often questioned whether I could persist with my initial stance. I considered and sometimes would quit, temporarily, while in my fight for my relationship with Jesus, with my husband, and just for life; but, I had this prayer, confession, and declaration that I held on to because I just knew that God heard me and could make it all possible.

During this process I said some very harsh things, made some very crazy choices, planned and plotted more horrible things, and didn't always have much sign of victory, but I kept confessing, believing, and telling God that I meant what I was praying no matter how much of a fool I was acting. I prayed, but then partially took vengeance into my own hands. I confessed the Word of God, but then cursed the people who hurt me. I stood, then fell, then got back up, then started all over again. I prayed and cried, then read God's Word and tried, over and over again. I listened to the preached Word on CDs, on my iPod, laptop, in my car, on airplanes, at my home, and in my hotel rooms. I went on fast after fast after fast. I thought I was overcoming, and then I'd have a bad day and get discouraged.

All throughout this process I kept adding to this prayer. I would rebuke myself for my thoughts and actions and then find the remedy to my problems in the Bible and add it to this prayer. I found everything in the Bible that I was supposed to say, have, and be, and would add it to this prayer, it seems like, daily. This prayer was my only way to remind myself of who God was, who I was, and who I had the potential to be in God, since my thoughts, actions, and reaction didn't always seem to reflect it. I told God if He'd allow this prayer to come to pass, I mean entirely, in the spirit and in the natural, I'd boldly tell the whole world that He changed my life and made me brand new.

Persevering and not losing heart was my greatest challenge through this process, but I knew I had two options: I could quit and/or give myself over to the anger, pain, and disappointment of my life, avenge myself but remain dissatisfied since I could not undo what had happened to me, wallow in sorrow while I qualified and justified it, and let the devil continue to defeat me and make me exist miserably,

OR, I could receive God's unconditional love and grace to accept and let go, fight the good fight of faith, pursue and have complete victory in Jesus, live a blessed and overcoming life, and declare God's greatness in the process. I chose the latter of the two and persevered.

I fell many days and got discouraged more often than I would have liked to, but I continued to pray and press and expect God to perform a miracle for me.

Truth is, the process looked like utter schizophrenia. I felt close to the devil because I failed, often and miserably, at being Christ like. I also felt closer to God than I ever had been in life because, on the days that I refused to yield to the overwhelming pressure of sorrow and evil thoughts, I ran to God so hard, so fast, so desperately, because I wanted Him and desperately wanted His Word to change me.

Sometimes I didn't see victory, but I confessed it. Sometimes I didn't feel victorious, but I confessed it. I got discouraged and fell but got back up and stood on the Word of God that I was reading, listening to, and confessing. Since God didn't allow my suicide attempts to work and didn't let me die some other way, which I begged for on many occasions, I decided I would fight and win and someday testify to the world about it.

Well, people, even against all these odds I continued to pray this prayer, read the Word of God, listen to the Word of God, and confess the Word of God over my life. I kept Jesus on my mind, in my heart, and in my mouth all day, every day, on good days and bad, and began to live with the expectation of having victory in every area of my life. I wanted a new life in Jesus Christ, and, well, I got it.

What you will continue to read are my personal conversations with my Savior. I pray that, in sharing these with you, they will encourage and bless you as much as they have blessed me, my husband, and my family.

.

I Believe

Gracious, loving, and faithful Father, I come to You right now acknowledging that You are the sovereign God of all creation. (**John 1:1-3** *In the beginning was the Word, and the Word was with God, and the Word was God. 2 The same was in the beginning with God. 3 All things were made by him; and without him was not any thing made that was made.* (**Genesis 1:1-31**).

You are the King of all kings and the Lord of all lords (**1 Timothy 6:15** *Which in his times he shall shew, who is the blessed and only Potentate, the King of kings, and Lord of lords*).

You are God of all gods (**Psalm 95:3** *For the Lord is a great God, and a great King above all gods*).

You are God in three persons: God the Father, God the Son, and God the Holy Spirit (**1 John 5:7** *For there are three that bear record in heaven, the Father, the Word, and the Holy Ghost: and these three are one;* **John 1:14** *And the Word was made flesh, and dwelt among us, (and we beheld his glory, the glory as of the only begotten of the Father, full of grace and truth;* **John 10:30** *I and My Father are one*).

I believe that You sent Your Son Jesus to save the world by dying on the cross for our sins (**John 3:16** *For God so loved the world*

*e His only begotten Son, that whosoever believeth in
! not perish, but have everlasting life*).

hat Jesus was resurrected from the dead after three
days a... He then ascended into heaven to sit on the right hand
of Your throne (**1 Corinthians 15:3-8** *For I delivered unto you
first of all that which I also received, how that Christ died for our
sins according to the Scriptures; 4 And that He was buried, and
that He rose again the third day according to the Scriptures; 5
And that He was seen of Cephas, then of the twelve. 6 After that,
he was seen of above five hundred brethren at once; of whom the
greater part remain unto this present, but some are fallen asleep.
7 After that, he was seen of James; then of all the apostles. 8 And
last of all He was seen of me also, as of one born out of due time;*
Acts 1:1-11 *The former treatise have I made, O Theophilus, of all
that Jesus began both to do and teach, 2 Until the day in which
he was taken up, after that he through the Holy Ghost had given
commandments unto the apostles whom he had chosen; 3 To whom
also he shewed himself alive after his passion by many infallible
proofs, being seen of them forty days, and speaking of the things
pertaining to the kingdom of God; 4 And, being assembled together
with them, commanded them that they should not depart from
Jerusalem, but wait for the promise for the Father, which, saith
he, ye have heard of me. 5 For John truly baptized with water; but
ye shall be baptized with the Holy Ghost not many days hence. 6
When they therefore were come together, they asked of him, saying,
Lord, wilt thou at this time restore again the kingdom to Israel? 7
And he said unto them, It is not for you to know the times or the
seasons, which the Father hath put in his own power. 8 But ye shall
receive power, after that the Holy Ghost is come upon you: and ye
shall be witnesses unto me both in Jerusalem, and in all Judaea,
and in Samaria, and unto the uttermost part of the earth. 9 And
when he had spoken these things, while they beheld, he was taken
up; and a cloud received him out of their sight. 10 And while they*

looked stedfastly toward heaven as he went up, behold, two men stood by them in white apparel; 11 Which also said, Ye men of Galilee, why stand ye gazing up into heaven? This same Jesus, which is taken up from you into heaven, shall so come in like manner as ye have seen him go into heaven).

I believe that He rose with the victory over death, sin, and over all of the powers of satan (**Ephesians 1:20-22** *which He wrought in Christ, when he raised him from the dead, and set him at his own right hand in the heavenly places, 21 Far above all principality, and power, and might, and dominion, and every name that is named, not only in this world, but also in that which is to come: 22 And He hath put all things under His feet, and gave Him to be the head over all things to the church.*

Colossians 2:14-15 *Blotting out the handwriting of ordinances that was against us, which was contrary to us, and took it out of the way, nailing it to his cross; 15 And having spoiled principalities and powers, he made a shew of them openly, triumphing over them in it).*

I believe that Jesus is my pathway to the Father, my way to access all that I am, and all that I have in God (**John 14:6** *Jesus saith unto him, I am the way, the truth, and the life: no man cometh unto the Father, but by Me).*

I believe that You, God, left the Holy Spirit after Jesus' ascension into heaven to help me in my Christian walk (**Acts1:8-9** *But ye shall receive power, after that the Holy Ghost has come upon you: and ye shall be witnesses unto me both in Jerusalem, and in all Judea, and in Samaria, and unto the uttermost part of the earth. 9 And when he had spoken these things, while they beheld, he was taken up; and a cloud received him out of their sight).*

I believe that You, God, are the only living God and the Holy Bible is the living Word (**Jeremiah 10:10** *But the Lord is the true*

God, he is the living God, and an everlasting King: at his wrath the earth shall tremble, and the nations shall not be able to abide his indignation; **Hebrews 4:12** *For the word of God is quick, and powerful, and sharper than any two-edged sword, piercing even to the dividing asunder of soul and spirit, and of the joints and marrow, and is a discerner of the thoughts and intents of the heart).*

I believe that You are the answer for everything and the Bible is the manual through which I come to know how to function and thrive in life, how to know the works, the will, and the voice of God, how to resist and defeat the devil, how to walk in authority and live victoriously, and be a true disciple of Jesus Christ (**2 Timothy 3:15-17** *15 And that from a child thou hast known the holy scriptures, which are able to make thee wise unto salvation through faith which is in Christ Jesus. 16 All scripture is given by inspiration of God, and is profitable for doctrine, for reproof, for correction, for instruction in righteousness: 17 that the man of God may be perfect, thoroughly furnished unto all good works).*

No one other than You can meet every spoken, unspoken, and even unaware need that I have, so Dear Heavenly Father, I come to Your throne of grace right now to find help because I am in need (**Hebrews 4:15-16** *For we have not an high priest who cannot be touched with the feeling of our infirmities; but was in all points tempted like as we are, yet without sin. 16 Let us therefore come boldly unto the throne of grace, that we may obtain mercy, and find grace to help in time of need).*

Ready For Change

Dear God, I am Your creation and You know me (**Psalm 139:13** *For thou hast possessed my reins: thou hast covered me in my mother's womb*).

You know how I think, how I work, what I feel, what I'm capable of, exactly what I need, and when I need it (**Psalm 139:1-4** *O lord, thou hast searched me, and known me. 2 Thou knowest my downsitting and mine uprising, Thou understandest my thought afar off. 3 Thou compasseth my path and my lying down, and art acquainted with all my ways. 4 For there is not a word in my tongue, but, lo, O Lord, thou knowest it altogether*).

I am ready for change that no one and nothing other than You can deliver (**Ezekiel 36:26-27** *A new heart also will I give you, and a new spirit will I put within you: and I will take the stony heart out of your flesh, and I will give you an heart of flesh. 27 And I will put my spirit within you, and cause you to walk in my statutes, and ye shall keep my judgments, and do them*). So, by faith, Lord, I confess this year to be my year of gratitude, optimism, rededication, maturation, complete deliverance, healing and restoration, knowledge, wisdom, revelation and illumination, increased capacity, and divine authority.

Gratitude

I thank You, Lord, for Your immense greatness (**Isaiah 40:21-22** *Have ye not known? have ye not heard? hath it not been told you from the beginning? have ye not understood from the foundations of the earth? 22 It is he that sitteth upon the circle of the earth, and the inhabitants thereof are as grasshoppers; that stretcheth out the heavens as a curtain, and spreadeth them out as a tent to dwell in;* **Isaiah 40:25-26** *To whom then will ye liken me, or shall I be equal?" saith the Holy One. 26 Lift up your eyes on high, and behold who hath created these things, that bringeth out their host by number: he calleth them all by names by the greatness of his might, for that he is strong in power; not one faileth;* **Jeremiah 10:12-13** *He hath made the earth by his power, he hath established the world by his wisdom, and hath stretched out the heavens by his discretion. 13 When he uttereth his voice, there is a multitude of waters in the heavens, and he causeth the vapors to ascend from the ends of the earth; he maketh lightnings with rain, and he bringeth forth the wind out of his treasures*).

I thank You for life, for allowing me to breathe Your air and experience the beauty of Your creation daily (**Psalm 118:24** *This is the day which the Lord hath made; we will rejoice and be glad in it*).

Lord, I understand that I was created to praise You, so I will bless You at all times and Your praises shall continually flow from my heart and mouth (**Psalm 34:1**).

I Confess My Sins

Lord, I confess every sin, known and unknown, that I have committed against You, myself, and anyone else.

I thank You for forgiving me of every sin, of everything that can or will block my prayers from being heard and answered (**1 John 1:9** *If we confess our sins, he is faithful and just to forgive us our sins, and to cleanse us from all unrighteousness*; **Psalm 66:18** *If I regard iniquity in my heart, the Lord will not hear me*).

God, I believe that You hear me, You will answer, and You will bring this prayer to pass (**1 John 5:14-15** *And this is the confidence that we have in him, that, if we ask any thing according to his will, he heareth us: 15 And if we know that he hear us, whatsoever we ask, we know that we have the petitions that we desired of him*).

Father, whenever or if ever my faith falters, I thank You for helping me to continue to believe (**Mark 9:23-24** *Jesus said unto him, "If thou canst believe, all things are possible to him that believeth." 24 And straightway the father of the child cried out, and said with tears, "Lord, I believe; help thou mine unbelief!"*).

Rededication

Lord, I have lived life selfishly and conveniently and I have attempted to take the matters of my life into my own hands. I don't want that type of existence anymore because it does not work (**1 John 5:12** *He that hath the Son hath life; and he that hath not the Son of God hath not life*; **John 15:5** *I am the vine, ye are the branches: He that abideth in me, and I in him, the same bringeth forth much fruit: for without me ye can do nothing*).

My sinful nature and instinctive learned behaviors make it so easy to be, act, and think the way I have in times past, but more challenging to take on my new identity in Christ, so I need You to help me, Father (**2 Corinthians 5:17** *Therefore if any man be in Christ, he is a new creature: old things are passed away; behold, all things are become new*; **Romans 7:18-23** *For I know that in me (that is, in my flesh,) dwelleth no good thing: for to will is present with me; but how to perform that which is good I find not. 19 For the good that I would, I do not; but the evil which I would not, that I do. 20 Now if I do that I would not, it is no more I that do it, but sin that dwelleth in me. 21 I find then a law, that, when I would do good, evil is present with me. 22 For I delight in the law of God after the inward man: 23 But I see another law in my members, warring against the law of my mind, and bringing me into captivity to the law of sin which is in my members*; **Hebrews 4:15-16** *For we have not an high* *priest which cannot be touched with the feeling of our infirmities; but was in all points tempted like as we are, yet without sin. 16 Let us therefore come boldly unto the throne of grace, that we may obtain mercy, and find grace to help in time of need).*

It is my desire to live a life that pleases You, Lord, so I come to You in total humility and I lay down every one of my burdens at Your feet (**Matthew 11:28-30** *Come unto me, all ye that labor and are heavy laden, and I will give you rest. 29 Take my yoke upon you, and learn of me; for I am meek and lowly in heart: and ye shall find rest unto your souls. 30 For my yoke is easy, and my burden is light*).

I cast the sum of my cares on You because I know that You care for me (**1 Peter 5:7**).

I surrender everything, totally and completely, to You, oh God, my Creator. I was created in Your image to be a reflection of Your image (**Genesis 1:27** *So God created man in his own image, in the image of God created he him; male and female created he them*) so I let go of everything that does not reflect You.

I am yielded to You completely (**Romans 6:16** *Know ye not, that to whom ye yield yourselves servants to obey, his servants ye are to whom ye obey; whether of sin unto death, or of obedience unto righteousness?* **Romans 6:19** *I speak after the manner of men because of the infirmity of your flesh: For as ye have yielded your members servants to uncleanness and to iniquity unto iniquity; even so now yield your members servants to righteousness unto holiness*).

Search me, oh God, and know my heart. Try me and know my thoughts. See if there be any wicked way in me and lead me along the path of everlasting life (**Psalm 139:23-24**).

I want my entire existence to glorify You (**Colossians 3:17** *And whatsoever ye do in word or deed, do all in the name of the Lord Jesus, giving thanks to God and the Father by him*).

I believe that Your plans for me are good, not evil, to give me hope and a prosperous future (**Jeremiah 29:11-13** *For I know the thoughts that I think toward you, saith the Lord, thoughts of peace, and not of evil, to give you an expected end. 12 Then shall ye call upon me, and ye shall go and pray unto me, and I will hearken unto you. 13 And ye shall seek me, and find me, when ye shall search for me with all your heart*) so I welcome You to assume Your rightful place in my life as Lord and Master (**John 13:13** *Ye call me Master and Lord: and ye say well; for so I am*).

Teach me Your commandments and I will obey them (**1 John 2:3** *And hereby we do know that we know him, if we keep his commandments*).

I forfeit my own will and desires and I ask You, Holy Spirit, to empower me to follow God's plan for my life (**Philippians 2:13** *For it is God which worketh in you both to will and to do of his good pleasure*; **John 14:26** *But the Comforter, which is the Holy Ghost, whom the Father will send in my name, He shall teach you all things, and bring all things to your remembrance, whatsoever I have said unto you*).

Revelation

God, I thank You for revealing Yourself to me daily. I confess and decree that I am lead by the Holy Spirit and God speaks to me (**1 John 2:20** *But ye have an unction from the Holy One, and ye know all things*; **John 10:27** *My sheep hear my voice, and I know them, and they follow me;* **John 16:13** *Howbeit when he, the Spirit of truth, is come, he will guide you into all truth: for he shall not speak of himself; but whatsoever he shall hear, that shall he speak: and he will shew you things to come*).

I confess and decree that I am increasing in the knowledge of the Word of God (**Ephesians 1:17-19** *That the God of our Lord Jesus Christ, the Father of glory, may give unto you the spirit of wisdom and revelation in the knowledge of Him: 18 The eyes of your understanding being enlightened; that ye may know what is the hope of his calling, and what the riches of the glory of his inheritance in the saints, 19 and what is the exceeding greatness of his power to us-ward who believe, according to the working of His mighty power*).

I understand that Jesus is the Word of God (**John 1:14** *And the Word was made flesh, and dwelt among us, and we beheld His glory, the glory as of the only begotten of the Father, full of grace and truth*) so I confess and decree that Jesus, the Word of God, is breathing life into me daily (**Proverbs 4:20-22** *My son, attend to my words; incline thine ear unto my sayings. 21 Let* *them not depart from thine eyes; keep them in the midst of thine heart. 22 For they are life unto those that find them, and health to all their flesh;* **Psalm 119:25** *My soul cleaveth unto the dust: quicken thou me according to thy word).*

I confess and decree that the mysteries of heaven are being unlocked to me (**Ephesians 1:9-11** *Having made known unto us the mystery of his will, according to his good pleasure which he hath purposed in himself: 10 That in the dispensation of the fullness of times he might gather together in one all things in Christ, both which are in heaven, and which are on earth; even in him: 11 In whom also we have obtained an inheritance, being predestinated according to the purpose of Him who worketh all things after the counsel of his own will;* **Colossians 1:26-27** *Even the mystery which hath been hid from ages and from generations, but now is made manifest to his saints: 27 To whom God would make known what is the riches of the glory of this mystery among the Gentiles; which is Christ in you, the hope of glory).*

I confess and decree that the Word of God is being sown in good soil and brings forth much fruit in my life (**Matthew 13:18-23** *Hear ye therefore the parable of the sower. 19 When any one heareth the word of the kingdom, and understandeth it not, then cometh the wicked one, and catcheth away that which was sown in his heart. This is he which receiveth seed by the way side. 20 But he that received the seed into stony places, the same is he that heareth the word, and anon with joy receiveth it; 21 Yet hath he not root in himself, but dureth for a while: for when tribulation or persecution ariseth because of the word, by and by he is offended.*

22 He also that received seed among the thorns is he that heareth the word; and the care of this world, and the deceitfulness of riches, choke the word, and he becometh unfruitful. 23 But he that received seed into the good ground is he that heareth the word, and understandeth it; which also beareth fruit, and bringeth

forth, some an hundredfold, some sixty, some thirty; **John 15:16**
*Ye have not chosen me, but I have chosen you, and ordained you,
that ye should go and bring forth fruit, and that your fruit should
remain: that whatsoever ye shall ask of the Father in my name,
he may give it you).*

Maturation, Knowledge, and Wisdom

God, I thank you for the discipline and the capacity to handle all that You have created me to be.

I thank You, Father, for making me bold, fearless, and persistent as I pursue becoming my greatest self (**1 Chronicles 28:20** *And David said to Solomon his son, Be strong and of good courage, and do it: fear not, nor be dismayed: for the Lord God, even my God, will be with thee; he will not fail thee, nor forsake thee, until thou hast finished all the work for the service of the house of the Lord*).

I thank You for balance (**Ecclesiastes 3:1-8** *To every thing there is a season, and a time to every purpose under the heaven:*

2 A time to be born, and a time to die; a time to plant, and a time to pluck up that which is planted;

3 A time to kill, and a time to heal; a time to break down, and a time to build up;

4 A time to weep, and a time to laugh; a time to mourn, and a time to dance;

5 A time to cast away stones, and a time to gather stones together; a time to embrace, and a time to refrain from embracing;

6 A time to get, and a time to lose; a time to keep, and a time to cast away;

7 A time to rend, and a time to sew; a time to keep silence, and a time to speak;

8 A time to love, and a time to hate; a time of war, and a time of peace.

I thank You that I am organized (**1 Corinthians 14:40** *Let all things be done decently and in order*).

I thank You that I am focused (**Ephesians 5:16** *Redeeming the time, because the days are evil*).

I thank You, God, for causing me to be a good listener and a great communicator (**James 1:19** *Wherefore, my beloved brethren, let every man be swift to hear, slow to speak, slow to wrath*).

I thank You, Lord, for causing me to hear counsel and receive instruction (**Proverbs 19:20** *Hear counsel, and receive instruction, that thou mayest be wise in thy latter end*).

I thank You for knowledge (**Proverbs 18:15** *The heart of the prudent getteth knowledge; And the ear of the wise seeketh knowledge*).

I thank You for wisdom and understanding (**Proverbs 3:13-20** *13 Happy is the man that findeth wisdom, and the man that getteth understanding. 14 For the merchandise of it is better than the merchandise of silver, and the gain thereof than fine gold. 15 She is more precious than rubies: and all the things thou canst desire are not to be compared unto her. 16 Length of days is in her right hand; and in her left hand riches and honour. 17 Her ways are ways of pleasantness, and all her paths are peace. 18 She is a tree of life to them that lay hold upon her: and happy is every one that retaineth her. 19 The Lord by wisdom hath founded the earth; by understanding hath he established the heavens. 20 By* his knowledge the depths are broken up, and the clouds drop down the dew; **James 1:**5 *If any of you lack wisdom, let him ask of God, that giveth to all men liberally, and upbraideth not; and it shall be given him).*

I thank You for great discernment and sound judgment (**Psalm 119:66** *Teach me good judgment and knowledge: for I have believed thy commandments;* **Philippians 1:9-10** *And this I pray, that your love may abound yet more and more in knowledge and in all judgment; 10 That ye may approve things that are excellent; that ye may be sincere and without offence till the day of Christ).*

I thank You for inner peace, contentment, and patience (**Philippians 4:11-12** *11 Not that I speak in respect of want: for I have learned, in whatsoever state I am, therewith to be content. 12 I know both how to be abased, and I know how to abound: every where and in all things I am instructed both to be full and to be hungry, both to abound and to suffer need;* **Hebrews 13:5-6** *Let your conversation be without covetousness; and be content with such things as ye have: for he hath said, I will never leave ye nor forsake thee. 6 So that we may boldly say, The Lord is my helper, and I will not fear what man shall do unto me;* **Psalm 37:7** *Rest in the Lord, and wait patiently for Him: fret not thyself because of him who prospereth in his way, because of the man who bringeth wicked devices to pass;* **Psalm 37:9** *For evildoers shall be cut off: but those that wait upon the Lord, they shall inherit the earth).*

God, I thank You for causing me to walk in Your love (**Ephesians 5:1-2** *Be ye therefore followers of God, as dear children; 2 And walk in love, as Christ also hath loved us, and hath given himself for us an offering and a sacrifice to God for a sweetsmelling savour;* **Matthew 5:44-48** *But I say unto you, Love your enemies, bless them that curse you, do good to them that hate you, and pray for them which despitefully use you, and persecute you; 45 That ye may be the children of your Father which is in heaven: for he maketh* *his sun to rise on the evil and on the good, and sendeth rain on the just and on the unjust. 46 For if ye love them which love you, what reward have ye? do not even the publicans the same? 47 And if ye salute your brethren only, what do ye more than others? do not even the publicans so? 48 Be ye therefore perfect, even as your Father which is in heaven is perfect).*

I thank You for causing me to be excellent (**Daniel 6:3** *Then this Daniel was preferred above the presidents and princes, because an excellent spirit was in him; and the king thought to set him over the whole realm*). And I thank You, Lord, for the diligence to finish well (**John 4:34** *Jesus saith unto them, My meat is to do the will of him that sent me, and to finish his work.*)

Increased Capacity

Now God, I thank You for an enhanced vision for my life personally, collectively with my husband/wife, professionally, and spiritually.

I thank You for causing me to know, accept, and fully occupy my place in Your Kingdom (**Ephesians 5:17** *Wherefore be ye not be unwise, but understanding what the will of the Lord is*).

I thank You for leading me to the path that helps me to fulfill my divine purpose and destiny (**Psalm 37:23** *The steps of a good man are ordered by the Lord: and he delighteth in his way;* **Psalm 1:1-3** *Blessed is the man that walketh not in the counsel of the ungodly, nor standeth in the way of sinners, nor sitteth in the seat of the scornful. 2 But his delight is in the law of the Lord; and in his law doth he meditate day and night. 3 And he shall be like a tree planted by the rivers of water, that bringeth forth his fruit in his season; his leaf also shall not wither; and whatsoever he doeth shall prosper*).

I decree that all things are working together for my good because I love You, Lord, and I am called according to Your purpose (**Romans 8:28**).

I decree that You are leading me to great advisors and You are leading great advisors to me for the benefit of accomplishing the purpose that You have ordained for my life (**Proverbs 15:22** *Without counsel purposes are disappointed: but in the multitude of counsellors they are established*).

Father, I thank You that my gifts make room for me and bring me before great people (**Proverbs 18:16**).

I thank You for causing those great men and women to use their power, influence, and other resources to help me.

I thank You for an expanded circle of friends and associates that are greater than me in some way; spiritually, intellectually, creatively, financially, politically.

Lord, I thank You for causing them to help inform me, push me, and stretch me to become greater than I am.

Father, I thank You for helping me to further discover and hone my inherent abilities.

I thank You for maximizing my potential (**Genesis 1:28** *And God blessed them, and God said unto them, Be fruitful, and multiply, and replenish the earth, and subdue it: and have dominion over the fish of the sea, and over the fowl of the air, and over every living thing that moveth upon the earth*; **Daniel 11:32** *And such as do wickedly against the covenant shall he corrupt by flatteries: but the people that do know their God shall be strong, and do exploits*). And Father, I thank You for causing me to see myself as You see me (**John 17:16-17** *They are not of the world, even as I am not of the world. 17 Sanctify them through thy truth: thy word is truth*; **John 17:21-26** *That they all may be one; as thou, Father, art in me, and I in thee, that they also may be one in us: that the world may believe that thou hast sent me. 22 And the glory which thou gavest me I have given them; that they may be one, even as we are one: 23 I in them, and thou in me, that they may be made perfect in one; and that the world may know that thou hast sent me, and* *hast loved them, as thou hast loved me. 24 Father, I will that they also, whom thou hast given me, be with me where I am; that they may behold my glory, which thou hast given me: for thou lovedst me before the foundation of the world. 25 O righteous Father, the world hath not known thee: but I have known thee, and these have known that thou hast sent me. 26 And I have declared unto them thy name, and will declare it: that the love wherewith thou hast loved me may be in them, and I in them).*

Healing In Marriage

Father, I confess and decree that my husband/wife and I are healed of all the hurt, pain, and disappointments of our past (**Psalm 147:3** *He healeth the broken in heart, and bindeth up their wounds*). You endured and carried our sorrow on the cross so we don't have to hold on to them (**Isaiah 53:4** *Surely he hath borne our griefs, and carried our sorrows: yet we did esteem him stricken, smitten of God, and afflicted*).

We refuse to keep account of or make mention of past offenses. They are history and they are forgiven (**Ephesians 4:31-32** *Let all bitterness, and wrath, and anger, and clamour, and evil speaking, be put away from you, with all malice: 32 And be ye kind one to another, tenderhearted, forgiving one another, even as God for Christ's sake hath forgiven you*; **Isaiah 43:25** *I, even I, am he that blotteth out thy transgressions for mine own sake, and will not remember thy sins*).

We let go of all of the unhealthy experiences and perspectives of our past as they diminish the joys of our present and ruin the hope of our future. We thank You for giving us beauty for ashes, joy for grief, and the Spirit of praise for the spirit of heaviness (**Isaiah 61:1, 3** *The Spirit of the Lord God is upon me; because the Lord hath anointed me to preach good tidings unto the meek; he hath sent me to bind up the brokenhearted, to proclaim liberty to the captives, and the opening of the prison to them that* *are bound; To appoint unto them that mourn in Zion, to give unto them beauty for ashes, the oil of joy for mourning, the garment of praise for the spirit of heaviness; that they might be called trees of righteousness, the planting of the Lord, that he might be glorified).* We thank You, Father, for a new and healthy view of our love and of each other.

Restoration

I confess and decree that my husband/wife and I have the greatest and truest love, honesty, trust, support, communication, understanding, consideration, friendship, unity, courtship, passion, pleasure, complete gratification, and overall commitment between two people that has ever been known to man. We thank You, Lord, for causing us to satisfy each other's total need for romantic love and intimacy. (**1 Corinthians 7:3-4** *Let the husband render unto the wife due benevolence: and likewise also the wife unto the husband. 4 The wife hath not power of her own body, but the husband: and likewise also the husband hath not power of his own body, but the wife;* **1 Corinthians 7:33-34** *But he that is married careth for the things that are of the world, how he may please his wife. 34 There is difference also between a wife and a virgin. The unmarried woman careth for the things of the Lord, that she may be holy both in body and in spirit: but she that is married careth for the things of the world, how she may please her husband*).

We thank You, Father, for teaching us to enjoy every facet of who we are individually and collectively.

We confess and decree that our marriage reflects every single thing that You intended it to.

We thank You for genuine and selfless love for each other. We thank You for committed and caring love for one another through better and worse, through richer and poorer, in sickness and in health, forsaking all others until death do us part (**Philippians 2:2-3** *Fulfil ye my joy, that ye be likeminded, having the same love, being of one accord, of one mind. 3 Let nothing be done through strife or vainglory; but in lowliness of mind let each esteem other better than themselves*).

Father, we thank You that all soul ties from every previous relationship and/or intimate encounter are broken right now, in the name of Jesus.

We thank You, Jesus, that Your blood cleanses us from all unrighteousness (**1 John 1:7, 9** *But if we walk in the light, as he is in the light, we have fellowship one with another, and the blood of Jesus Christ his Son cleanseth us from all sin*). We thank You that Your blood is even powerful enough to remove all residue and remembrance of sin in our past (**Psalm 103:12** *As far as the east is from the west, so far hath he removed our transgressions from us;* **Micah 7:18-19** *Who is a God like unto thee, that pardoneth iniquity, and passeth by the transgression of the remnant of his heritage? he retaineth not his anger for ever, because he delighteth in mercy*).

We thank You that all thoughts of, memories of, and appetites for any other man or woman are removed from us and never returns again.

We thank You, Father, for the willingness to risk exposing all aspects of our being to each other in exchange for the opportunity to truly become one and gain everything that love and marriage has to offer (**Mark 10:8** *And they twain shall be one flesh: so then they are no more twain, but one flesh;* **Ephesians 4:3-4** *Endeavouring to keep the unity of the Spirit in the bond of* *peace. 4 There is one body, and one Spirit, even as ye are called in one hope of your calling;* **Ephesians 5:3** *But fornication, and all uncleanness, or covetousness, let it not be once named among you, as becometh saints).* God, we thank You that we have an honorable marriage that only glorifies You (**Hebrews 13:4** *Marriage is honorable in all, and the bed undefiled: but whoremongers and adulterers God will judge*).

Marriage Built On Biblical Principles

Father, Your Word establishes that wives should submit to their husband's authority and reverence him. Your Word also establishes that husbands should love their wives as Christ loved the church and gave His life for it (**1 Peter 3:1-7** *Likewise, ye wives, be in subjection to your own husbands; that, if any obey not the word, they also may without the word be won by the conversation of the wives; 2 While they behold your chaste conversation coupled with fear. 3 Whose adorning let it not be that outward adorning of plaiting the hair, and of wearing of gold, or of putting on of apparel; 4 But let it be the hidden man of the heart, in that which is not corruptible, even the ornament of a meek and quiet spirit, which is in the sight of God of great price. 5 For after this manner in the old time the holy women also, who trusted in God, adorned themselves, being in subjection unto their own husbands: 6 Even as Sara obeyed Abraham, calling him lord: whose daughters ye are, as long as ye do well, and are not afraid with any amazement.*

7 Likewise, ye husbands, dwell with them according to knowledge, giving honour unto the wife, as unto the weaker vessel, and as being heirs together of the grace of life; that your prayers be not hindered.; **Ephesians 5:22-29** *Wives, submit yourselves unto your own husbands, as unto the Lord. 23 For the husband is the head of the wife, even as Christ is the head of the church: and he* *is the saviour of the body. 24 Therefore as the church is subject unto Christ, so let the wives be to their own husbands in every thing. 25 Husbands, love your wives, even as Christ also loved the church, and gave himself for it; 26 That he might sanctify and cleanse it with the washing of water by the word, 27 That he might present it to himself a glorious church, not having spot, or wrinkle, or any such thing; but that it should be holy and without blemish. 28 So ought men to love their wives as their own bodies. He that loveth his wife loveth himself. 29 For no man ever yet hated his own flesh; but nourisheth and cherisheth it, even as the Lord the church).*

We thank You that this is established in our relationship now and forever.

We thank You, Father, for making us greater together than we will ever be apart (**Ecclesiastes 4:9-12** *Two are better than one; because they have a good reward for their labour. 10 For if they fall, the one will lift up his fellow: but woe to him that is alone when he falleth; for he hath not another to help him up. 11 Again, if two lie together, then they have heat: but how can one be warm alone? 12 And if one prevail against him, two shall withstand him; and a threefold cord is not quickly broken).*

We thank You, Father, that divorce is not an option in this marriage so the discussion of such will never be entertained (**Mark 10:9** *What therefore God hath joined together, let not man put asunder).*

We thank You for the willingness to rectify all disagreements or conflict in our relationship before our day ends (**Ephesians 4:26** *Be ye angry, and sin not: let not the sun go down upon your wrath).*

We confess and decree that we will give envy and strife no place in this relationship (**James 3:16** *For where envying and strife is, there is confusion and every evil work).*

We confess and decree that we use kind words to deflect frustration and anger (**Proverbs 15:1** *A soft answer turneth away wrath: but grievous words stir up anger*; **Proverbs 16:24** *Pleasant words are as an honeycomb, sweet to the soul, and health to the bones*).

We confess and decree that we will live harmoniously and love each other with the unconditional love of Christ (**Romans 12:16-18** *Be of the same mind one toward another. Mind not high things, but condescend to men of low estate. Be not wise in your own conceits. 17 Recompense to no man evil for evil. Provide things honest in the sight of all men. 18 If it be possible, as much as lieth in you, live peaceably with all men*; **1 Corinthians 13:4-8** *Charity suffereth long, and is kind; charity envieth not; charity vaunteth not itself, is not puffed up, 5 Doth not behave itself unseemly, seeketh not her own, is not easily provoked, thinketh no evil; 6 Rejoiceth not in iniquity, but rejoiceth in the truth; 7 Beareth all things, believeth all things, hopeth all things, endureth all things. 8 Charity never faileth: but whether there be prophecies, they shall fail; whether there be tongues, they shall cease; whether there be knowledge, it shall vanish away*).

We thank You, Father, that our family prays together and will stay together, happily and lovingly, through the submission to Your Word and the leadership of my husband/myself (**Psalm 127:1** *Except the Lord build the house, they labour in vain that build it: except the Lord keep the city, the watchman waketh but in vain*; **Proverbs 24:3-4** *Through wisdom is an house builded; and by understanding it is established: 4 And by knowledge shall the chambers be filled with all precious and pleasant riches*; **1 Corinthians 11:3** *But I would have you know, that the head of every man is Christ; and the head of the woman is the man; and the head of Christ is God*).

We declare and decree that the glory of our future will be greater than that of our past (**Haggai 2:9** *The glory of this house shall* *be greater than of the former, saith the Lord of hosts: and in this place will I give peace, saith the Lord of hosts;* **Isaiah 43:18-19** *Remember ye not the former things, neither consider the things of old. 19 Behold, I will do a new thing; now it shall spring forth; shall ye not know it? I will even make a way in the wilderness, and rivers in the desert).*

Prayer for My Spouse

God, I thank You for my husband's/wife's enhanced vision for himself/herself personally, collectively with me, professionally, and spiritually.

Father, I thank You for the immediate manifestation of his/her strength, discipline, and capacity to handle all that this vision entails.

I thank You, God, for giving my husband/wife supernatural confidence and fearlessness in his/her pursuit of fulfilling his/her divine purpose and destiny and becoming his/her best in every aspect of his/her existence (**1 Chronicles 28:20** *And David said to Solomon his son, Be strong and of good courage, and do it: fear not, nor be dismayed: for the Lord God, even my God, will be with thee; he will not fail thee, nor forsake thee, until thou hast finished all the work for the service of the house of the Lord*).

I thank You for causing him/her to know, accept, and fully occupy his/her place in Your Kingdom (**Ephesians 5:17** *Wherefore be ye not unwise, but understanding what the will of the Lord is*).

I confess and decree that You have made him/her a whole and perfected man/woman in Christ Jesus (**Colossians 2:9-10** *For in him dwelleth all the fulness of the Godhead bodily. 10 And ye are complete in him, which is the head of all principality and power*).

I thank You for helping him/her to further discover and hone his/her inherent abilities. I thank You for maximizing his/her potential (**Daniel 11:32** *And such as do wickedly against the covenant shall he corrupt by flatteries: but the people that do know their God shall be strong, and do exploits*).

Father, I thank You for causing me to consistently acknowledge his/her strengths and love him/her through his/her shortcomings knowing that love covers many faults (**1 Peter 4:8** *And above all things have fervent charity among yourselves: for charity shall cover the multitude of sins*).

God, I thank You for causing me to see my husband/wife as You see him/her (**John 17:16** *They are not of the world, even as I am not of the world. **John 17:21-26** That they all may be one; as thou, Father, art in me, and I in thee, that they also may be one in us: that the world may believe that thou hast sent me. 22 And the glory which thou gavest me I have given them; that they may be one, even as we are one: 23 I in them, and thou in me, that they may be made perfect in one; and that the world may know that thou hast sent me, and hast loved them, as thou hast loved me. 24 Father, I will that they also, whom thou hast given me, be with me where I am; that they may behold my glory, which thou hast given me: for thou lovedst me before the foundation of the world. 25 O righteous Father, the world hath not known thee: but I have known thee, and these have known that thou hast sent me. 26 And I have declared unto them thy name, and will declare it: that the love wherewith thou hast loved me may be in them, and I in them*).

I confess and decree that I will do him/her good and not evil all the days of my life (**Proverbs 31:11-12** *The heart of her husband doth safely trust in her, so that he shall have no need of spoil. 12 She will do him good and not evil all the days of her life*).

Bless Our Family

Father, we thank You that Your blood covers our marriage, our children, and our family. We decree and declare that we and our entire house will serve You, Lord (**Joshua 24:15** *And if it seem evil unto you to serve the Lord, choose you this day whom ye will serve; whether the gods which your fathers served that were on the other side of the flood, or the gods of the Amorites, in whose land ye dwell: but as for me and my house, we will serve the Lord*).

We thank You for causing us to wake each day with God on our minds, praise on our lips, and love and gratitude in our hearts.

We thank You for causing us to regularly notice the goodness and mercy that follows us every day of our lives (**Psalm 23:6** *Surely goodness and mercy shall follow me all the days of my life: and I will dwell in the house of the Lord forever*).

We thank You for Your great provision of safety for us (**Psalm 121:5-8** *The Lord is thy keeper: the Lord is thy shade upon thy right hand. 6 The sun shall not smite thee by day, nor the moon by night. 7 The Lord shall preserve thee from all evil: he shall preserve thy soul. 8 The Lord shall preserve thy going out and thy coming in from this time forth, and even for evermore*).

We thank You for causing us to walk in divine health and to prosper even as our souls prosper (**Psalm 91:10** *There shall no*

evil befall thee, neither shall any plague come nigh thy dwelling;
3 John 1:2; **Proverbs 3:7-8** *Be not wise in thine own eyes: fear the Lord, and depart from evil. 8 It shall be health to thy navel, and marrow to thy bones; Fear the Lord and depart from evil. 8 It will be health to your flesh, And strength to your bones).*

We thank You for helping us to be present in the moments and experiences of our lives (**James 4:14** *Whereas ye know not what shall be on the morrow. For what is your life? It is even a vapour, that appeareth for a little time, and then vanisheth away;* **Ecclesiastes 5:18-20** *Behold that which I have seen: it is good and comely for one to eat and to drink, and to enjoy the good of all his labour that he taketh under the sun all the days of his life, which God giveth him: for it is his portion. 19 Every man also to whom God hath given riches and wealth, and hath given him power to eat thereof, and to take his portion, and to rejoice in his labour; this is the gift of God. 20 For he shall not much remember the days of his life; because God answereth him in the joy of his heart).*

We thank You, Jesus, for giving us all life and life more abundantly (**John 10:10** *The thief cometh not, but for to steal, and to kill, and to destroy: I am come that they might have life, and that they might have it more abundantly).*

We thank You for helping us train our children in the way that they should go so that even when they get older, they will not depart from it (**Proverbs 22:6**).

We thank You that as a result of us training them, You will cause our children to be lovers of God and disciples of Christ (**Deuteronomy 30:6** *And the Lord thy God will circumcise thine heart, and the heart of thy seed, to love the Lord thy God with all thine heart, and with all thy soul, that thou mayest live).*

God, our children are a gift from You so we thank You for them (**Psalm 127:3-4** *Lo, children are an heritage of the Lord: and the* *fruit of the womb is his reward. 4 As arrows are in the hand of a mighty man; so are children of the youth).*

We confess and decree that they are happy, loving, honest, obedient, respectful, responsible, capable, confident, and intelligent, with winning dispositions.

Father God, in the name of Jesus, we decree that our children will reach their fullest potential in every aspect of their existence and they will become exactly who You have created them to be (**Philippians 4:13** *I can do all things through Christ which strengtheneth me).*

We thank You for causing our children to honor us and thereby live long lives (**Ephesians 6:2-3** *Honour thy father and mother; which is the first commandment with promise; 3 That it may be well with thee, and thou mayest live long on the earth).*

Lord, I confess and decree that I am blessed, my husband/wife is blessed, our marriage is blessed, our home is blessed, our children are blessed, our children's children are blessed, and their children are blessed (**Ephesians 1:3** *Blessed be the God and Father of our Lord Jesus Christ, who hath blessed us with all spiritual blessings in heavenly places in Christ;* **Psalm 112:1-3** *Praise ye the Lord. Blessed is the man that feareth the Lord, that delighteth greatly in his commandments. 2 His seed shall be mighty upon earth: the generation of the upright shall be blessed. 3 Wealth and riches shall be in his house: and his righteousness endureth for ever;* **Deuteronomy 7:9** *Know therefore that the Lord thy God, he is God, the faithful God, which keepeth covenant and mercy with them that love him and keep his commandments to a thousand generations).*

I decree that my husband/wife and I will leave an inheritance to our children, to their children, and to their children's children (**Proverbs 13:22** *A good man leaveth an inheritance to his* *children's children: and the wealth of the sinner is laid up for the just*).

Lord, we thank You for causing us to be great examples of love, concern, support, patience, attentiveness, understanding, enthusiasm, wisdom, excellence, integrity, and godliness to our children (**Matthew 7:12** *Therefore all things whatsoever ye would that men should do to you, do ye even so to them: for this is the law and the prophets*).

Return on Investment

Father, I confess and decree that my husband/wife and I are Your righteousness and that the wealth of the sinner is stored up for the righteous (**Proverbs 13:22** *A good man leaveth an inheritance to his children's children: and the wealth of the sinner is laid up for the just*).

We confess and decree that You are showing us how to find that wealth, create that wealth, sustain that wealth, and use that wealth to build Your Kingdom and make Your name greater in this earth.

We thank You that the wealth that we do not find, finds us.

We thank You for favor with You, and favor with men (**Proverbs 3:4** *So shalt thou find favour and good understanding in the sight of God and man*).

We thank You, Father, that poverty is not Your will for our lives and recessions do not affect us because You shall supply our every need according to Your riches in glory (**Philippians 4:19** *But my God shall supply all your need according to his riches in glory by Christ Jesus*).

We confess and decree that, because we are tithers, the windows of heaven have been opened to pour us out a blessing that we do not even have enough room to receive (**Malachi 3:10** *Bring* *ye all the tithes into the storehouse, that there may be meat in mine house, and prove me now herewith, saith the Lord of hosts, if I will not open you the windows of heaven, and pour you out a blessing, that there shall not be room enough to receive it;* **Proverbs 3:9-10** *Honour the Lord with thy substance, and with the firstfruits of all thine increase: 10 So shall thy barns be filled with plenty, and thy presses shall burst out with new wine).*

We confess and decree that this year and each consecutive year of our lives You are causing our tithes and offerings to be multiplied unto us exponentially, and ALL nations will call us blessed as a result (**Malachi 3:11-12** *And I will rebuke the devourer for your sakes, and he shall not destroy the fruits of your ground; neither shall your vine cast her fruit before the time in the field, saith the Lord of hosts. 12 And all nations shall call you blessed: for ye shall be a delightsome land, saith the Lord of hosts).*

Blessed Finances

Father God, we believe that the blessing of the Lord makes us rich and adds no sorrow (**Proverbs 10:22**), so my husband/wife and I confess and decree that we are blessed by the best and full of joy because of it.

We further confess and decree that all of our bills are paid on time, all of our debt is cancelled, and we will remain debt free.

As we walk in righteousness and pursue a life that brings glory to God and builds the Kingdom of God, we thank You, Father, that Your supernatural provision is adding everything that we need to us (**Matthew 6:33** *But seek ye first the kingdom of God, and his righteousness; and all these things shall be added unto you*).

We receive Your supernatural insight to develop and implement all of our creative ideas and abilities that generate immense wealth (**Deuteronomy 8:18** *But thou shalt remember the Lord thy God: for it is he that giveth thee power to get wealth, that he may establish his covenant which he sware unto thy fathers, as it is this day*).

We are exceedingly wise in financial matters (**Isaiah 48:17** *Thus saith the Lord, thy Redeemer, the Holy One of Israel; I am the Lord thy God which teacheth thee to profit, which leadeth thee by the way that thou shouldest go;* **Proverbs 21:5** *The thoughts* *of the diligent tend only to plenteousness; but of every one that is hasty only to want).*

Every seed that we sow multiplies and receives the maximum return (**Luke 6:38** *Give, and it shall be given unto you; good measure, pressed down, and shaken together, and running over, shall men give into your bosom. For with the same measure that ye mete withal it shall be measured to you again).*

We are lenders, not borrowers. We are the head, not the tail. We are above, and not beneath (**Deuteronomy 28:12-13** *The Lord shall open unto thee his good treasure, the heaven to give the rain unto thy land in his season, and to bless all the work of thine hand: and thou shalt lend unto many nations, and thou shalt not borrow. 13 And the Lord shall make thee the head, and not the tail; and thou shalt be above only, and thou shalt not be beneath; if that thou hearken unto the commandments of the Lord thy God, which I command thee this day, to observe and to do them).*

We sow willfully and bountifully, we reap bountifully, and we have more than enough to sow into the needs of God's people and into the work of the Lord (**2 Corinthians 9:6-8** *But this I say, He which soweth sparingly shall reap also sparingly; and he which soweth bountifully shall reap also bountifully. 7 Every man according as he purposeth in his heart, so let him give; not grudgingly, or of necessity: for God loveth a cheerful giver. 8 And God is able to make all grace abound toward you; that ye, always having all sufficiency in all things, may abound to every good work;* **Deuteronomy 15:10-11** *Thou shalt surely give him, and thine heart shall not be grieved when thou givest unto him: because that for this thing the Lord thy God shall bless thee in all thy works, and in all that thou puttest thine hand unto. 11 For the poor shall never cease out of the land: therefore I command thee, saying, Thou shalt open thine hand wide unto thy brother, to thy poor, and to thy needy, in thy land).*

Our giving is founded on Biblical principle; therefore, the great success of our seed is inevitable (**Joshua 1:8** *This book of the law shall not depart out of thy mouth; but thou shalt meditate therein day and night, that thou mayest observe to do according to all that is written therein: for then thou shalt make thy way prosperous, and then thou shalt have good success).* The blessing of the Lord, it maketh rich, and he addeth no sorrow with it.

We command financial prosperity to be ours.

We declare and decree that our harvest time is now.

Father, in the name of Jesus, we come together, touching and agreeing for what we have asked and what we have prayed for, with full confidence that we shall receive it from You (**Matthew 18:19-20** *Again I say unto you, That if two of you shall agree on earth as touching any thing that they shall ask, it shall be done for them of my Father which is in heaven. 20 For where two or three are gathered together in my name, there am I in the midst of them).*

Complete Deliverance

Father God, in the name of Jesus, I confess and decree that every stronghold that has attached itself to my being, and every generational curse that has been passed down through the sins of any and every one in my bloodline, are broken right now.

Father, You said in Your word that Jesus Christ has redeemed me from the curse of the law of sin and death when He was hung on the tree, rather, the cross (**Galatians 3:13-29** *Christ hath redeemed us from the curse of the law, being made a curse for us: for it is written, Cursed is every one that hangeth on a tree: 14 That the blessing of Abraham might come on the Gentiles through Jesus Christ; that we might receive the promise of the Spirit through faith. 15 Brethren, I speak after the manner of men; Though it be but a man's covenant, yet if it be confirmed, no man disannulleth, or addeth thereto. 16 Now to Abraham and his seed were the promises made. He saith not, And to seeds, as of many; but as of one, And to thy seed, which is Christ. 17 And this I say, that the covenant, that was confirmed before of God in Christ, the law, which was four hundred and thirty years after, cannot disannul, that it should make the promise of none effect. 18 For if the inheritance be of the law, it is no more of promise: but God gave it to Abraham by promise. 19 Wherefore then serveth the law? It was added because of transgressions, till the seed should come to whom the promise was made; and it was ordained by angels in the hand* *of a mediator. 20 Now a mediator is not a mediator of one, but God is one. 21 Is the law then against the promises of God? God forbid: for if there had been a law given which could have given life, verily righteousness should have been by the law. 22 But the scripture hath concluded all under sin, that the promise by faith of Jesus Christ might be given to them that believe. 23 But before faith came, we were kept under the law, shut up unto the faith which should afterwards be revealed. 24 Wherefore the law was our schoolmaster to bring us unto Christ, that we might be justified by faith. 25 But after that faith is come, we are no longer under a schoolmaster. 26 For ye are all the children of God by faith in Christ Jesus. 27 For as many of you as have been baptized into Christ have put on Christ. 28 There is neither Jew nor Greek, there is neither bond nor free, there is neither male nor female: for ye are all one in Christ Jesus. 29 And if ye be Christ's, then are ye Abraham's seed, and heirs according to the promise).*

According to Your word, I am, therefore, dead to curses and sin, and I am alive to righteousness (**Romans 8:2-10** *For the law of the Spirit of life in Christ Jesus hath made me free from the law of sin and death. 3 For what the law could not do, in that it was weak through the flesh, God sending his own Son in the likeness of sinful flesh, and for sin, condemned sin in the flesh: 4 That the righteousness of the law might be fulfilled in us, who walk not after the flesh, but after the Spirit. 5 For they that are after the flesh do mind the things of the flesh; but they that are after the Spirit the things of the Spirit. 6 For to be carnally minded is death; but to be spiritually minded is life and peace. 7 Because the carnal mind is enmity against God: for it is not subject to the law of God, neither indeed can be. 8 So then they that are in the flesh cannot please God. 9 But ye are not in the flesh, but in the Spirit, if so be that the Spirit of God dwell in you. Now if any man have not the Spirit of Christ, he is none of his. 10 And if Christ be in you, the body is dead because of sin; but the Spirit is life because of righteousness).*

I have been purified by means of a blood transfusion with Jesus' blood that He shed on the cross (**Colossians 1:20-21** *And, having made peace through the blood of his cross, by him to reconcile all things unto himself; by him, I say, whether they be things in earth, or things in heaven. 21 And you, that were sometime alienated and enemies in your mind by wicked works, yet now hath he reconciled;* **1 John 1:7** *But if we walk in the light, as he is in the light, we have fellowship one with another, and the blood of Jesus Christ his Son cleanseth us from all sin*).

So Father God, in the name of Jesus, I take authority over anger, frustration, rage, vengeance, insecurity, anxiety, faithlessness, fear, jealousy, envy, bitterness, resentment, contention, rebellion, selfishness, loneliness, rejection, shame, emotionalism, depression, oppression, unforgiveness, pride, complaining, lying, evil speaking, sexual perversion, idolatry, greed, discontentment, sadness, sickness and disease, lack, ungodly practices, and ungodly mindsets; I command all these mountains to be removed and cast into outer darkness (**Romans 6:5-6** *For if we have been planted together in the likeness of his death, we shall be also in the likeness of his resurrection: 6 Knowing this, that our old man is crucified with him, that the body of sin might be destroyed, that henceforth we should not serve sin;* **Romans 6:12-14** *Let not sin therefore reign in your mortal body, that ye should obey it in the lusts thereof. 13 Neither yield ye your members as instruments of unrighteousness unto sin: but yield yourselves unto God, as those that are alive from the dead, and your members as instruments of righteousness unto God. 14 For sin shall not have dominion over you: for ye are not under the law, but under grace;* **Mark 11:23** *For verily I say unto you, That whosoever shall say unto this mountain, Be thou removed, and be thou cast into the sea; and shall not doubt in his heart, but shall believe that those things which he saith shall come to pass; he shall have whatsoever he saith*).

I cast down all reasoning and every high-minded thing that exalts itself against the knowledge of God, and I command every thought to be obedient to the knowledge of Christ (**2 Corinthians 10:4-5** *For the weapons of our warfare are not carnal, but mighty through God to the pulling down of strong holds; 5 Casting down imaginations, and every high thing that exalteth itself against the knowledge of God, and bringing into captivity every thought to the obedience of Christ*).

This mental battle with the devil's lies and deception has lasted far too long, so satan, I command you to shut up and leave right now, in the name of Jesus (**Acts 16:16-18** *And it came to pass, as we went to prayer, a certain damsel possessed with a spirit of divination met us, which brought her masters much gain by soothsaying:17 The same followed Paul and us, and cried, saying, These men are the servants of the most high God, which shew unto us the way of salvation. 18 And this did she many days. But Paul, being grieved, turned and said to the spirit, I command thee in the name of Jesus Christ to come out of her. And he came out the same hour*).

Devil, you don't have an advantage over me because I am aware of your devices (**2 Corinthians 11:3** *But I fear, lest by any means, as the serpent beguiled Eve through his subtilty, so your minds should be corrupted from the simplicity that is in Christ;* **2 Corinthians 2:11** *Lest Satan should get an advantage of us: for we are not ignorant of his devices*). But, no weapon formed against me shall prosper (**Isaiah 54:17** *No weapon that is formed against thee shall prosper; and every tongue that shall rise against thee in judgment thou shalt condemn. This is the heritage of the servants of the Lord, and their righteousness is of me, saith the Lord*).

I am strong in You, Lord, and in Your mighty power. I put on the full armor of God to be able to stand firm against the devil's strategies, and after I've done all that I can do, I will continue to stand and put on my belt of truth, my breastplate of righteousness, the gospel of peace, the shield of faith, the helmet of salvation, the sword of the Spirit which is the Word of God, and I will always pray in the Spirit to fight the enemy, pull down every stronghold, and destroy the devil's plan concerning me (**Ephesians 6:10-18** *Finally, my brethren, be strong in the Lord, and in the power of his might. 11 Put on the whole armour of God, that ye may be able to stand against the wiles of the devil. 12 For we wrestle not against flesh and blood, but against principalities, against powers, against the rulers of the darkness of this world, against spiritual wickedness in high places. 13 Wherefore take unto you the whole armour of God, that ye may be able to withstand in the evil day, and having done all, to stand. 14 Stand therefore, having your loins girt about with truth, and having on the breastplate of righteousness; 15 And your feet shod with the preparation of the gospel of peace; 16 Above all, taking the shield of faith, wherewith ye shall be able to quench all the fiery darts of the wicked. 17 And take the helmet of salvation, and the sword of the Spirit, which is the word of God: 18 Praying always with all prayer and supplication in the Spirit, and watching thereunto with all perseverance and supplication for all saints*).

I approach life courageously knowing that You are with me and You are for me and, if God be for me, who can be against me (**Joshua 1:9** *Have not I commanded thee? Be strong and of a good courage; be not afraid, neither be thou dismayed: for the Lord thy God is with thee whithersoever thou goest;* **Romans 8:31-32** *What shall we then say to these things? If God be for us, who can be against us? 32 He that spared not his own Son, but delivered him up for us all, how shall he not with him also freely give us all things?*)?

The Spirit of the living God that is inside of me is greater than anything in the world (**1 John 4:4** *Ye are of God, little children,* *and have overcome them: because greater is he that is in you, than he that is in the world).*

The Lord will defeat every one of my enemies. They will come against me one way, and flee from me in seven ways (**Deuteronomy 28:7** *The Lord shall cause thine enemies that rise up against thee to be smitten before thy face: they shall come out against thee one way, and flee before thee seven ways).*

Lord, You make me as surefooted as a deer to walk over the mountainous challenges in my life (**Habakkuk 3:19** *The Lord God is my strength, and he will make my feet like hinds' feet, and he will make me to walk upon mine high places.*).

I decree that I overcome by the blood of the Lamb and by the word of my testimony (**Revelation 12:10-11** *And I heard a loud voice saying in heaven, Now is come salvation, and strength, and the kingdom of our God, and the power of his Christ: for the accuser of our brethren is cast down, which accused them before our God day and night. 11 And they overcame him by the blood of the Lamb, and by the word of their testimony; and they loved not their lives unto the death).*

I fight the good fight of faith and I win (**1 Timothy 6:12** *Fight the good fight of faith, lay hold on eternal life, whereunto thou art also called, and hast professed a good profession before many witnesses).*

The Truth Makes Me Free

I thank God that the blood of Jesus has cleansed my heart and mind so that I can effectively serve the living God (**Hebrews 9:14** *How much more shall the blood of Christ, who through the eternal Spirit offered himself without spot to God, purge your conscience from dead works to serve the living God?*).

I now hide Your Word in my heart, oh God, so that I will not sin against You (**Psalm 119:11** *Thy word have I hid in mine heart, that I might not sin against thee*).

I confess and decree that You have replaced all sin in my life with the fruit of the Spirit which is love, joy, peace, long suffering, gentleness, goodness, faith, meekness, and temperance or self-control (**Galatians 5:22-25** *But the fruit of the Spirit is love, joy, peace, longsuffering, gentleness, goodness, faith, 23 Meekness, temperance: against such there is no law. 24 And they that are Christ's have crucified the flesh with the affections and lusts. 25 If we live in the Spirit, let us also walk in the Spirit*).

I thank You, Jesus, for liberating me and changing me (**John 8:32** *And ye shall know the truth, and the truth shall make you free*; **2 Corinthians 3:17-18** *Now the Lord is that Spirit: and where the Spirit of the Lord is, there is liberty. 18 But we all, with open face beholding as in a glass the glory of the Lord, are*

*changed into the same image from glory to glory, even as by the ·
Spirit of the Lord).*

Lord, I thank You for godly people in my life who hold me
accountable to the truth of Your Word (**Philippians 2:2** *Fulfil
ye my joy, that ye be likeminded, having the same love, being of
one accord, of one mind*).

I thank You, Lord, for a heart to pursue Your presence because
in Your presence our spirits connect and everything contrary
to You disconnects (**Hebrews 10:22** *Let us draw near with a
true heart in full assurance of faith, having our hearts sprinkled
from an evil conscience, and our bodies washed with pure water;*
Psalm 16:11 *Thou wilt shew me the path of life: in thy presence
is fulness of joy; at thy right hand there are pleasures for evermore*).

My New Existence

I thank You, Father, for the eyes to see, the ears to hear, the wisdom to perceive, and a heart to receive Your spiritual truths. I thank You, Jesus, for the power to overcome the triggers that lead me out of Your will. I thank You for new responses and new reactions to old problems and old triggers.

I thank You, Father, that I consider Your Word above and beyond all that happens in my life today and every day. I now live in Christ, so I am a new person (**2 Corinthians 5:17-21** *Therefore if any man be in Christ, he is a new creature: old things are passed away; behold, all things are become new. 18 And all things are of God, who hath reconciled us to himself by Jesus Christ, and hath given to us the ministry of reconciliation; 19 To wit, that God was in Christ, reconciling the world unto himself, not imputing their trespasses unto them; and hath committed unto us the word of reconciliation. 20 Now then we are ambassadors for Christ, as though God did beseech you by us: we pray you in Christ's stead, be ye reconciled to God. 21 For he hath made him to be sin for us, who knew no sin; that we might be made the righteousness of God in him.*) The old me no longer exists.

I thank You, Father, for showing me in Your Word that the same Spirit that raised Jesus from the dead is alive in me (**Romans 8:11** *But if the Spirit of him that raised up Jesus from the dead* *dwell in you, he that raised up Christ from the dead shall also quicken your mortal bodies by his Spirit that dwelleth in you).*

I receive the complete transference of all my new birth rites as an heir of God and a joint heir with Christ (**Romans 8:14-17** *For as many as are led by the Spirit of God, they are the sons of God. 15 For ye have not received the spirit of bondage again to fear; but ye have received the Spirit of adoption, whereby we cry, Abba, Father. 16 The Spirit itself beareth witness with our spirit, that we are the children of God: 17 And if children, then heirs; heirs of God, and joint-heirs with Christ; if so be that we suffer with him, that we may be also glorified together).*

I thank You, Father, for helping me to walk in the Spirit so that I do not fulfill the lust of the flesh (**Galatians 5:16**). I command my body and soul to come into alignment with the spiritual transformation that God has brought about in my life.

I confess and decree that I will give no space to the devil (**Ephesians 4:27** *Neitherr give place to the devil).*

Lord, I receive Your grace, Your unmerited favor, to walk in this newness of life (**Acts 20:32** *And now, brethren, I commend you to God, and to the word of his grace, which is able to build you up, and to give you an inheritance among all them which are sanctified).* Jesus, You overcame the world and because I believe in You, I, too, overcome the world. (**1 John 5:4-5** *For whatsoever is born of God overcometh the world: and this is the victory that overcometh the world, even our faith. 5 Who is he that overcometh the world, but he that believeth that Jesus is the Son of God)?*

I am a walking, breathing, living, modern day example of Your miraculous power and love. I am Your workmanship, recreated in Christ Jesus for good works (**Ephesians 2:10** *For we are his workmanship, created in Christ Jesus unto good works, which God hath before ordained that we should walk in them).*

You chose me and called me out of darkness into Your marvelous light (**Ephesians 1:4-6** *According as he hath chosen us in him before the foundation of the world, that we should be holy and without blame before him in love: 5 Having predestinated us unto the adoption of children by Jesus Christ to himself, according to the good pleasure of his will, 6 To the praise of the glory of his grace, wherein he hath made us accepted in the beloved;* **1 Peter 2:9** *But ye are a chosen generation, a royal priesthood, an holy nation, a peculiar people; that ye should shew forth the praises of him who hath called you out of darkness into his marvellous light*).

I am united with Jesus and seated in heavenly places (**Ephesians 2:4-7** *But God, who is rich in mercy, for his great love wherewith he loved us, 5 Even when we were dead in sins, hath quickened us together with Christ, (by grace ye are saved;)*

6 And hath raised us up together, and made us sit together in heavenly places in Christ Jesus: 7 That in the ages to come he might shew the exceeding riches of his grace in his kindness toward us through Christ Jesus).

I am forgetting the things behind me and reaching forward to what is ahead (**Philippians 3:13-14** *Brethren, I do not count myself to have apprehended; but one thing I do, forgetting those things which are behind and reaching forward to those things which are ahead, 14 I press toward the goal for the prize of the upward call of God in Christ Jesus*).

I press toward the mark for the prize of the upward call of God in Christ Jesus, being fully confident that He who has begun a good work in me is able to and will complete it (**Philippians 1:6** *Being confident of this very thing, that he which hath begun a good work in you will perform it until the day of Jesus Christ*).

I will live a holy, acceptable life unto You, Lord, which is my reasonable service (**Romans 12:1** *I beseech you therefore, brethren,* *by the mercies of God, that ye present your bodies a living sacrifice, holy, acceptable unto God, which is your reasonable service).*

The God of peace that brought the Lord Jesus from the dead through the everlasting blood covenant makes me perfect in every good work to do His will, working in me that which is well pleasing in His sight, through Jesus Christ (**Hebrews 13:20-21**).

The Blood of Jesus and Angelic Hosts Cover My Family

Father God, I apply the blood of Jesus and command all generational curses to immediately be broken over my husband's/ wife's and my children's lives. All curses, hexes, witchcraft, forms of satanic professions and/or demonic activity or influence and warfare, past, present, and/or future, on, over, or toward my family, are broken, cast into outer darkness, and commanded to never return again, in the mighty name of Jesus.

Father, Your Word declares that You have given me power to trample serpents and scorpions and over all the powers of the enemy and that nothing shall by any means hurt me, so I use that power to trample on all the powers of darkness (**Luke 10:19** *Behold, I give unto you power to tread on serpents and scorpions, and over all the power of the enemy: and nothing shall by any means hurt you*). You have given me the keys of Your Kingdom, the power to bind and loose, so I use my God given authority to bind bloodline curses, generational strongholds, and all the powers of satan and his cohorts and I command my husband/wife, myself, and my children to be loosed from all powers, influences, and effects of darkness in the mighty name of Jesus (**Matthew 16:19** *And I will give unto thee the keys of the kingdom of heaven: and whatsoever thou shalt bind on*

*earth shall be bound in heaven: and whatsoever thou shalt loose
on earth shall be loosed in heaven).*

I release the overcoming power of the blood of Jesus and the
unyielding strength of the Almighty God and His angelic host
over me and my family right now and just as the blood caused
the plagues in the Old Testament to bypass certain homes and
be of no effect (**Exodus 12:13** *And the blood shall be to you for
a token upon the houses where ye are: and when I see the blood, I
will pass over you, and the plague shall not be upon you to destroy
you, when I smite the land of Egypt*), I apply the blood of Jesus
over my husband/wife, myself, my children, our home, and our
surroundings and I command every assignment of the enemy
concerning any and/or all of us, collectively and/or individually,
to be cancelled immediately and rendered of no effect.

Satan, I break your power right now in the name of Jesus and
I disallow every single one of your plans concerning us. Jesus'
work on the cross annihilated your plans (**1 John 3:8** *He that
committeth sin is of the devil; for the devil sinneth from the beginning. For this purpose the Son of God was manifested, that he might
destroy the works of the devil*), so devil, you can't have us; we
belong to God (**John 10:28-29** *And I give unto them eternal life;
and they shall never perish, neither shall any man pluck them out
of my hand. 29 My Father, which gave them me, is greater than
all; and no man is able to pluck them out of my Father's hand*).

Arise, oh God, and let Your enemies be scattered (**Psalm 68:1**
*Let God arise, let his enemies be scattered: let them also that hate
him flee before him*).

I thank You, Father, that You and Your angelic host encamps
around about me, my husband/wife, our children, our home,
and everywhere that we may be, to save us from harm (**Psalm**

34:7 *The angel of the Lord encampeth round about them that fear him, and delivereth them).*

I command every hindrance to God's will being manifested in our lives and every hindrance to God's outpouring of blessings in our lives, to be removed, in the name of Jesus. I ask, Father God, that You would send forth Your angels that have been assigned to me, my husband/wife, and our children, to war on our behalf and retrieve every blessing that You have for all of us individually and collectively (**Psalm 91:11-16** *For he shall give his angels charge over thee, to keep thee in all thy ways. 12 They shall bear thee up in their hands, lest thou dash thy foot against a stone 13 Thou shalt tread upon the lion and adder: the young lion and the dragon shalt thou trample under feet. 14 Because he hath set his love upon me, therefore will I deliver him: I will set him on high, because he hath known my name. 15 He shall call upon me, and I will answer him: I will be with him in trouble; I will deliver him, and honour him. 16 With long life will I satisfy him, and shew him my salvation;* **Psalms 103:21** *Bless ye the Lord, all ye his hosts; ye ministers of his, that do his pleasure).*

Renounce Every Accursed Word

Now, Father God, I renounce every accursed word, at its very root, that I have ever spoken that did not line up with the Word of God for my life, for my family's life, and for the lives of whomever I was speaking to or about.

I command every one of those lifeless and/or idle words to fall to the ground and die right now, in the name of Jesus.

I reject words of death and I choose life this very moment (**Deuteronomy 30:19** *I call heaven and earth to record this day against you, that I have set before you life and death, blessing and cursing: therefore choose life, that both thou and thy seed may live;* **Proverbs 18:20-21** *A man's belly shall be satisfied with the fruit of his mouth; and with the increase of his lips shall he be filled. 21 Death and life are in the power of the tongue: and they that love it shall eat the fruit thereof*).

I fully revoke my entitlement to negative words, feelings, thoughts, actions, reactions, and memories brought about through unfavorable life experiences. Father God, in the name of Jesus, I command my thoughts, my emotions, my spirit, my practices, and my words to immediately line up with Your plan for my life. Let the words of my mouth and the meditation of my heart be acceptable in Thy sight, oh Lord, my strength and my redeemer (**Psalm 19:14**). You keep guard over my mouth and teach me to speak words of kindness and wisdom (**Psalm 141:3** *Set a watch, O Lord, before my mouth; keep the door of my lips*; **Proverbs 31:26** *She openeth her mouth with wisdom; and in her tongue is the law of kindness*). I speak the will of the Lord (**2 Corinthians 4:13** *We having the same spirit of faith, according as it is written, I believed, and therefore have I spoken; we also believe, and therefore speak*).

Satan, you are crushed under my feet (**Romans 16:20** *And the God of peace shall bruise Satan under your feet shortly. The grace of our Lord Jesus Christ be with you. Amen*). I declare and decree victory over my life in every area of my life (**1 Corinthians 15:57** *But thanks be to God, which giveth us the victory through our Lord Jesus Christ*).

I Confess and Decree That I Am

I confess and decree that I am everything that the Word of God says.

I am forgiven (**Isaiah 55:7** *Let the wicked forsake his way, and the unrighteous man his thoughts: and let him return unto the Lord, and he will have mercy upon him; and to our God, for he will abundantly pardon*).

I am redeemed (**Titus 2:14** *Who gave himself for us, that he might redeem us from all iniquity, and purify unto himself a peculiar people, zealous of good works*).

I am accepted (**Ephesians 1:4-6** *According as he hath chosen us in him before the foundation of the world, that we should be holy and without blame before him in love: 5 Having predestinated us unto the adoption of children by Jesus Christ to himself, according to the good pleasure of his will, 6 To the praise of the glory of his grace, wherein he hath made us accepted in the beloved*).

I am delivered (**Colossians 1:13** *Who hath delivered us from the power of darkness, and hath translated us into the kingdom of his dear Son*).

I am not condemned (**Romans 8:1** *There is therefore now no condemnation to them which are in Christ Jesus, who walk not after the flesh, but after the Spirit*).

I am justified (**Romans 5:1** *Therefore being justified by faith, we have peace with God through our Lord Jesus Christ*).

I have confessed with my mouth that Jesus is Lord, and I believe that God has raised Jesus from the dead; therefore, I am saved (**Romans 10:9-10** *That if thou shalt confess with thy mouth the Lord Jesus, and shalt believe in thine heart that God hath raised him from the dead, thou shalt be saved. 10 For with the heart man believeth unto righteousness; and with the mouth confession is made unto salvation*).

I have been saved by grace through faith. I could not and did not earn it. It is my gift from God (**Ephesians 2:8-9** *For by grace are ye saved through faith; and that not of yourselves: it is the gift of God: 9 Not of works, lest any man should boast*).

I have been made righteous (**2 Corinthians 5:21** *For he hath made him to be sin for us, who knew no sin; that we might be made the righteousness of God in him*).

My spirit is one with Christ (**1 Corinthians 6:17** *But he that is joined unto the Lord is one spirit*).

I am whole (**James 1:4** *But let patience have her perfect work, that ye may be perfect and entire, wanting nothing*).

I am healed (**Isaiah 53:5** *But he was wounded for our transgressions, he was bruised for our iniquities: the chastisement of our peace was upon him; and with his stripes we are healed*).

I am holy, unblameable, and unreprovable (**Colossians 1:21-22** *And you, that were sometime alienated and enemies in your mind by wicked works, yet now hath he reconciled 22 In the body of his flesh through death, to present you holy and unblameable and unreproveable in his sight*).

God has created in me a clean heart and renewed a right spirit within me (**Psalm 51:10** *Create in me a clean heart, O God; and renew a right spirit within me*).

God is my mind regulator so I have a sound mind (**2 Timothy 1:7** *For God hath not given us the spirit of fear; but of power, and of love, and of a sound mind*).

I think on the things that are true, honest, just, pure, lovely, virtuous, praiseworthy, and of good report (**Philippians 4:8** *Finally, brethren, whatsoever things are true, whatsoever things are honest, whatsoever things are just, whatsoever things are pure, whatsoever things are lovely, whatsoever things are of good report; if there be any virtue, and if there be any praise, think on these things*).

I am anxious for nothing but, for every aspect of my existence, with prayer and petitions, I make my request known to You, Lord. Your peace guards my heart and mind (**Philippians 4:6-7** *Be careful for nothing; but in every thing by prayer and supplication with thanksgiving let your requests be made known unto God. 7 And the peace of God, which passeth all understanding, shall keep your hearts and minds through Christ Jesus*).

I am being transformed by renewing my mind daily so that I may prove what is the good and acceptable and perfect will of God (**Romans 12:2** *And be not conformed to this world: but be ye transformed by the renewing of your mind, that ye may prove what is that good, and acceptable, and perfect, will of God*). I have the mind of Christ (**Philippians 2:5** *Let this mind be in you, which was also in Christ Jesus*).

I am loved by Almighty God with a perfect love that casts out all of my fears (**1 John 4:10** *Herein is love, not that we loved God, but that he loved us, and sent his Son to be the propitiation for our sins; **1 John 4:18** *There is no fear in love; but perfect love casteth out fear: because fear hath torment. He that feareth is not made* *perfect in love*). This love caused You, Father, to send Your only begotten Son, Jesus, to give His life on the cross in exchange for my everlasting life. (**John 3:16** *For God so loved the world, that he gave his only begotten Son, that whosoever believeth in him should not perish, but have everlasting life*).

Thank You, Jesus! There is nothing that can separate me from Your love (**Romans 8:35** *Who shall separate us from the love of Christ? shall tribulation, or distress, or persecution, or famine, or nakedness, or peril, or sword?*; **Romans 8:38-39** *For I am persuaded, that neither death, nor life, nor angels, nor principalities, nor powers, nor things present, nor things to come, 39 Nor height, nor depth, nor any other creature, shall be able to separate us from the love of God, which is in Christ Jesus our Lord*).

I thank You for helping me comprehend how wide, how long, how high, and how deep this love is for me (**Ephesians 3:17-19** *That Christ may dwell in your hearts by faith; that ye, being rooted and grounded in love, 18 May be able to comprehend with all saints what is the breadth, and length, and depth, and height; 19 And to know the love of Christ, which passeth knowledge, that ye might be filled with all the fulness of God*).

You have given me a loving spirit (**2 Timothy 1:7** *For God hath not given us the spirit of fear; but of power, and of love, and of a sound mind*). As You perfect Your love in me, I have confidence in my ability to live as You lived on this earth (**1 John 4:17** *Herein is our love made perfect, that we may have boldness in the day of judgment: because as he is, so are we in this world*).

You have given me peace (**John 14:27** *Peace I leave with you, my peace I give unto you: not as the world giveth, give I unto you. Let not your heart be troubled, neither let it be afraid*).

I have Your joy inside of me (**John 15:10-11** *If ye keep my commandments, ye shall abide in my love; even as I have kept my*

Father's commandments, and abide in his love. 11 These things have I spoken unto you, that my joy might remain in you, and that your joy might be full).

I have compassion, consideration, and respect for others (**1 Corinthians 12:25-26** *That there should be no schism in the body; but that the members should have the same care one for another. 26 And whether one member suffer, all the members suffer with it; or one member be honoured, all the members rejoice with it;* **Romans 12:10** *Be kindly affectioned one to another with brotherly love; in honour preferring one another).*

I look beyond people's flaws and I choose to see the good in them. I show mercy because You have shown me mercy (**Psalm 107:1** *O give thanks unto the Lord, for he is good: for his mercy endureth for ever).*

I will love others as You have loved me (**John 15:12** *This is my commandment, That ye love one another, as I have loved you).*

I walk in humility (**James 4:10** *Humble yourselves in the sight of the Lord, and he shall lift you up;* **Philippians 2:3-4** *Let nothing be done through strife or vainglory; but in lowliness of mind let each esteem other better than themselves. 4 Look not every man on his own things, but every man also on the things of others),* yet I am capable and confident because I can do all things through Jesus Christ who strengthens me (**Philippians 4:** *I can do all things through Christ which strengtheneth me).*

I am growing in grace (**2 Peter 1:2** *Grace and peace be multiplied unto you through the knowledge of God, and of Jesus our Lord).*

I have a teachable spirit (**Proverbs 9:9** *Give instruction to a wise man, and he will be yet wiser: teach a just man, and he will increase in learning).*

I am being perfected daily by the Word of God, knowing that God has given me all things that pertain to life and godliness (**2 Timothy 3:16-17** *All scripture is given by inspiration of God, and is profitable for doctrine, for reproof, for correction, for instruction in righteousness: 17 That the man of God may be perfect, thoroughly furnished unto all good works;* **2 Peter 1:2-8** *Grace and peace be multiplied unto you through the knowledge of God, and of Jesus our Lord, 3 According as his divine power hath given unto us all things that pertain unto life and godliness, through the knowledge of him that hath called us to glory and virtue: 4 Whereby are given unto us exceeding great and precious promises: that by these ye might be partakers of the divine nature, having escaped the corruption that is in the world through lust. 5 And beside this, giving all diligence, add to your faith virtue; and to virtue knowledge; 6 And to knowledge temperance; and to temperance patience; and to patience godliness; 7 And to godliness brotherly kindness; and to brotherly kindness charity. 8 For if these things be in you, and abound, they make you that ye shall neither be barren nor unfruitful in the knowledge of our Lord Jesus Christ*).

God Authors My Faith

God, You are the author and the finisher of my faith (**Hebrews 12:1-3** *Wherefore seeing we also are compassed about with so great a cloud of witnesses, let us lay aside every weight, and the sin which doth so easily beset us, and let us run with patience the race that is set before us, 2 Looking unto Jesus the author and finisher of our faith; who for the joy that was set before him endured the cross, despising the shame, and is set down at the right hand of the throne of God. 3 For consider him that endured such contradiction of sinners against himself, lest ye be wearied and faint in your minds*).

I decrease daily so that You might increase in me (**John 3:30** *He must increase, but I must decrease*).

I fear You and no one else and in You, oh God, do I put my trust (**Psalm 56:11** *In God have I put my trust: I will not be afraid what man can do unto me*).

I will not avenge myself. God avenges me (**Romans 12:19** *Dearly beloved, avenge not yourselves, but rather give place unto wrath: for it is written, Vengeance is mine; I will repay, saith the Lord*).

I will not be overcome by evil, but I will overcome evil with good (**Romans 12:21**)

I will keep praying, praising, worshiping, hearing Your Word, reading Your Word, and standing on Your Word as I journey through this life in Christ (**Hebrews 12:28** *Wherefore we receiving a kingdom which cannot be moved, let us have grace, whereby we may serve God acceptably with reverence and godly fear*; **Hebrews13:15** *By him therefore let us offer the sacrifice of praise to God continually, that is, the fruit of our lips giving thanks to his name*; **Romans 10:17** *So then faith cometh by hearing, and hearing by the word of God*; **Job 23:**12 *Neither have I gone back from the commandment of his lips; I have esteemed the words of his mouth more than my necessary food*).

I will not quit. I will not faint in the face of adversity (**Proverbs 24:10** *If thou faint in the day of adversity, thy strength is small*).

I will wait on You, Lord, and be courageous, knowing that You will strengthen me (**Psalm 27:13-14** *I had fainted, unless I had believed to see the goodness of the Lord in the land of the living. 14 Wait on the Lord: be of good courage, and he shall strengthen thine heart: wait, I say, on the Lord*; **Psalm 46:1** *God is our refuge and strength, a very present help in trouble*), knowing that Your grace is sufficient for me, knowing that Your strength is made perfect in my weakness (**2 Corinthians 12:9-10** *And he said unto me, My grace is sufficient for thee: for my strength is made perfect in weakness. Most gladly therefore will I rather glory in my infirmities, that the power of Christ may rest upon me. 10 Therefore I take pleasure in infirmities, in reproaches, in necessities, in persecutions, in distresses for Christ's sake: for when I am weak, then am I strong*), knowing that You will cause me to soar, (**Isaiah 40:28-31** *Hast thou not known? hast thou not heard, that the everlasting God, the Lord, the Creator of the ends of the earth, fainteth not, neither is weary? There is no searching of his understanding. 29 He giveth power to the faint; and to them that have no might he increaseth strength. 30 Even the youths shall faint and be weary, and the young men shall utterly fall: 31 But they that wait upon the Lord shall renew their strength; they shall* mount up with wings as eagles; they shall run, and not be weary; and they shall walk, and not faint).

I resist the devil and he flees from me (**James 4:7** *Submit yourselves therefore to God. Resist the devil, and he will flee from you*).

I set my affections on things above, not on things on earth (**Colossians 3:1-2** *If ye then be risen with Christ, seek those things which are above, where Christ sitteth on the right hand of God. 2 Set your affection on things above, not on things on the earth*).

I hunger and thirst after righteousness and I thank You, Lord, that I am being filled as a result (**Matthew 5:6** *Blessed are they which do hunger and thirst after righteousness: for they shall be filled*).

I study the Word of God so that I may know the Word of God and live according to the will of God (**James 1:21-25** *Wherefore lay apart all filthiness and superfluity of naughtiness, and receive with meekness the engrafted word, which is able to save your souls. 22 But be ye doers of the word, and not hearers only, deceiving your own selves. 23 For if any be a hearer of the word, and not a doer, he is like unto a man beholding his natural face in a glass: 24 For he beholdeth himself, and goeth his way, and straightway forgetteth what manner of man he was. 25 But whoso looketh into the perfect law of liberty, and continueth therein, he being not a forgetful hearer, but a doer of the work, this man shall be blessed in his deed*). I am a disciple of Christ (**John 8:31** *Then said Jesus to those Jews which believed on him, If ye continue in my word, then are ye my disciples indeed*). I thank You, Jesus, for a heart and mind that is fixed on You, for I know that I manifest the sum of my thoughts (**Proverbs 23:7** *For as a man thinketh in his heart, so is he.*).

Divine Authority

Lord, I thank You for an acute awareness that I was discipled by You to be a light that shines for You and to do greater works in this earth (**Matthew 5:14-16** *Ye are the light of the world. A city that is set on a hill cannot be hid. 15 Neither do men light a candle, and put it under a bushel, but on a candlestick; and it giveth light unto all that are in the house. 16 Let your light so shine before men, that they may see your good works, and glorify your Father which is in heaven;* **John 14:12-14** *Verily, verily, I say unto you, He that believeth on me, the works that I do shall he do also; and greater works than these shall he do; because I go unto my Father. 13 And whatsoever ye shall ask in my name, that will I do, that the Father may be glorified in the Son. 14 If ye shall ask any thing in my name, I will do it;* **Mark 16:15** *And he said unto them, Go ye into all the world, and preach the gospel to every creature,* **Mark 16:18** *They shall take up serpents; and if they drink any deadly thing, it shall not hurt them; they shall lay hands on the sick, and they shall recover*).

I thank God that I have the faith of Jesus Christ, and I release my faith to operate in the supernatural power of Jesus Christ (**Galatians 2:20** *I am crucified with Christ: nevertheless I live; yet not I, but Christ liveth in me: and the life which I now live in the flesh I live by the faith of the Son of God, who loved me, and*

gave himself for me; **Hebrews 11:3-35** ; **1 Corinthians 4:20**
For the kingdom of God is not in word, but in power).

I thank You, Jesus, that as I walk in faith and declare Your truths,
You are with me even until the end of the earth (**Matthew
28:18-20** *And Jesus came and spake unto them, saying, All power
is given unto me in heaven and in earth. 19 Go ye therefore, and
teach all nations, baptizing them in the name of the Father, and
of the Son, and of the Holy Ghost: 20 Teaching them to observe
all things whatsoever I have commanded you: and, lo, I am with
you always, even unto the end of the world. Amen).*

I am not nor will I be intimidated by or concerned with the
opinions of others regarding my faith in God (**1 Corinthians
15:33** *Be not deceived: evil communications corrupt good manners).*

I seek the honor of God, not of people (**John 5:44** *How can
ye believe, which receive honour one of another, and seek not the
honour that cometh from God only?*; **1 Thessalonians 2:4** *But as
we were allowed of God to be put in trust with the gospel, even so
we speak; not as pleasing men, but God, which trieth our hearts).*

I am secure in Him alone. I have the faith to do anything
because I believe the Holy Bible and I reject unbelief (**Romans
4:3** *For what saith the scripture? Abraham believed God, and it
was counted unto him for righteousness;* **Romans 4: 18-22** *Who
against hope believed in hope, that he might become the father of
many nations, according to that which was spoken, So shall thy seed
be. 19 And being not weak in faith, he considered not his own body
now dead, when he was about an hundred years old, neither yet
the deadness of Sarah's womb: 20 He staggered not at the promise
of God through unbelief; but was strong in faith, giving glory to
God; 21 And being fully persuaded that, what he had promised,
he was able also to perform. 22 And therefore it was imputed to
him for righteousness;* **Mark 9:24** *And straightway the father of*

the child cried out, and said with tears, Lord, I believe; help thou mine unbelief).

I refuse to be double-minded (**James 1:6-8** *But let him ask in faith, nothing wavering. For he that wavereth is like a wave of the sea driven with the wind and tossed. 7 For let not that man think that he shall receive any thing of the Lord. 8 A double minded man is unstable in all his ways*).

I only believe (**Luke 8:50** *But when Jesus heard it, he answered him, saying, Fear not: believe only, and she shall be made whole*).

I thank You, Holy Spirit, that I am alert to the enemy working against this mission (**1 Peter 5:8** *Be sober, be vigilant; because your adversary the devil, as a roaring lion, walketh about, seeking whom he may devour;* **John 10:10** *The thief cometh not, but for to steal, and to kill, and to destroy: I am come that they might have life, and that they might have it more abundantly*).

I understand that my struggle is not against flesh and blood but against principalities and powers and rulers of the darkness of this world, against spiritual wickedness in high places (**Ephesians 6:12** *For we wrestle not against flesh and blood, but against principalities, against powers, against the rulers of the darkness of this world, against spiritual wickedness in high places*). So Lord, I thank You for causing me to pray without ceasing, for I know that You hear me, and I know that my sincere, effectual prayers accomplish much (**1 Thessalonians 5:16-18** *Rejoice evermore. 17 Pray without ceasing. 18 In every thing give thanks: for this is the will of God in Christ Jesus concerning you;* **Psalm 55:17** *Evening, and morning, and at noon, will I pray, and cry aloud: and he shall hear my voice;* **James 5:16** *Confess your faults one to another, and pray one for another, that ye may be healed. The effectual fervent prayer of a righteous man availeth much*).

I thank You that when I pray, You show me great and mighty things (**Jeremiah 33:3** *Call unto me, and I will answer thee, and show thee great and mighty things, which thou knowest not*).

I thank You that You show Yourself mighty on my behalf (**2 Chronicles 16:9** *For the eyes of the Lord run to and fro throughout the whole earth, to shew himself strong in the behalf of them whose heart is perfect toward him.*).

I thank You that Your power comes in like a raging flood tide to overtake every attack of the devil (**Isaiah 59:19** *So shall they fear the name of the Lord from the west, and his glory from the rising of the sun. When the enemy shall come in like a flood, the Spirit of the Lord shall lift up a standard against him*; **Deuteronomy 28:7** *The Lord shall cause thine enemies that rise up against thee to be smitten before thy face: they shall come out against thee one way, and flee before thee seven ways*).

I thank You for the power that is in Your name Jesus (**James 2:19** *Thou believest that there is one God; thou doest well: the devils also believe, and tremble*; **Luke 10:17** *And the seventy returned again with joy, saying, Lord, even the devils are subject unto us through thy name*).

I submit wholly to Your great name (**Philippians 2:9-11** *Wherefore God also hath highly exalted him, and given him a name which is above every name: 10 That at the name of Jesus every knee should bow, of things in heaven, and things in earth, and things under the earth; 11 And that every tongue should confess that Jesus Christ is Lord, to the glory of God the Father*).

I thank You, Jesus, that through You I conquer every single thing that I face (**Romans 8:37** *Nay, in all these things we are more than conquerors through him that loved us*).

I do nothing of my own strength and wisdom. I rely totally on Jesus, my solid rock, who has all wisdom and all power, who wins every battle (**1 Samuel 2:2-10** *There is none holy as the Lord: for there is none beside thee: neither is there any rock like our God. 3 Talk no more so exceeding proudly; let not arrogancy come out of your mouth: for the Lord is a God of knowledge, and by him actions are weighed. 4 The bows of the mighty men are broken, and they that stumbled are girded with strength. 5 They that were full have hired out themselves for bread; and they that were hungry ceased: so that the barren hath born seven; and she that hath many children is waxed feeble. 6 The Lord killeth, and maketh alive: he bringeth down to the grave, and bringeth up. 7 The Lord maketh poor, and maketh rich: he bringeth low, and lifteth up. 8 He raiseth up the poor out of the dust, and lifteth up the beggar from the dunghill, to set them among princes, and to make them inherit the throne of glory: for the pillars of the earth are the Lord's, and he hath set the world upon them. 9 He will keep the feet of his saints, and the wicked shall be silent in darkness; for by strength shall no man prevail. 10 The adversaries of the Lord shall be broken to pieces; out of heaven shall he thunder upon them: the Lord shall judge the ends of the earth; and he shall give strength unto his king, and exalt the horn of his anointed*).

You are my God and I am Your servant; I will not be discouraged because You help me and uphold me with Your right hand (**Isaiah 41:10** *Fear thou not; for I am with thee: be not dismayed; for I am thy God: I will strengthen thee; yea, I will help thee; yea, I will uphold thee with the right hand of my righteousness*).

I thank You, Father, for always causing me to triumph because of Christ Jesus (**2 Corinthians 2:14** *Now thanks be unto God, which always causeth us to triumph in Christ, and maketh manifest the savour of his knowledge by us in every place*).

Thank You, Jesus

Thank You, Jesus, for every experience that has made me who I am. Thank You, Jesus, for every experience that has helped me to understand and appreciate who You are. Thank You, Jesus, for the challenges in my life that brought me closer to You (**Psalm 119:71** *It is good for me that I have been afflicted; that I might learn thy statutes;* **Isaiah 30:20-21** *And though the Lord give you the bread of adversity, and the water of affliction, yet shall not thy teachers be removed into a corner any more, but thine eyes shall see thy teachers: 21 And thine ears shall hear a word behind thee, saying, This is the way, walk ye in it, when ye turn to the right hand, and when ye turn to the left*).

Thank You, Jesus, for the greatness that is being birthed out of my tribulations (**Romans 5:3-5** *And not only so, but we glory in tribulations also: knowing that tribulation worketh patience; 4 And patience, experience; and experience, hope:*

5 And hope maketh not ashamed; because the love of God is shed abroad in our hearts by the Holy Ghost which is given unto us; **Isaiah 48:10-11** *Behold, I have refined thee, but not with silver; I have chosen thee in the furnace of affliction. 11 For mine own sake, even for mine own sake, will I do it: for how should my name be polluted? And I will not give my glory unto another*).

Thank You, Jesus, for Your faithfulness toward me (**Psalm 36:5** *Thy mercy, O Lord, is in the heavens; and thy faithfulness reacheth unto the clouds*).

To You, oh God, be the glory for all the things that You have done (**1 Samuel 12:24** *Only fear the Lord, and serve him in truth with all your heart: for consider how great things he hath done for you*).

Glory to God

God, my Father, I exalt Your name in this earth (**Psalm 118:28** *Thou art my God, and I will praise thee: thou art my God, I will exalt thee*). I exalt Your name high above the heavens.

You are great and greatly to be praised (**Psalm 48:1** *Great is the Lord, and greatly to be praised in the city of our God, in the mountain of his holiness*).

I magnify You, Great God, beyond every problem, circumstance, and situation that I have faced and will face.

You are holy (**1 Samuel 2:2** *There is none holy as the Lord: for there is none beside thee: neither is there any rock like our God*).

You are sovereign. Your power and greatness extend to the ends of the universe (**Isaiah 40:21-26** *Have ye not known? have ye not heard? hath it not been told you from the beginning? have ye not understood from the foundations of the earth? 22 It is he that sitteth upon the circle of the earth, and the inhabitants thereof are as grasshoppers; that stretcheth out the heavens as a curtain, and spreadeth them out as a tent to dwell in: 23 That bringeth the princes to nothing; he maketh the judges of the earth as vanity. 24 Yea, they shall not be planted; yea, they shall not be sown: yea, their stock shall not take root in the earth: and he shall also blow upon them, and they shall wither, and the whirlwind shall take* *them away as stubble. 25 To whom then will ye liken me, or shall I be equal? saith the Holy One. 26 Lift up your eyes on high, and behold who hath created these things, that bringeth out their host by number: he calleth them all by names by the greatness of his might, for that he is strong in power; not one faileth).*

You, Father God, are paramount to everyone and everything (**Colossians 1:16-17** *For by him were all things created, that are in heaven, and that are in earth, visible and invisible, whether they be thrones, or dominions, or principalities, or powers: all things were created by him, and for him: 17 And he is before all things, and by him all things consist*).

You are Alpha and Omega *(***Revelation 1:8** *I am Alpha and Omega, the beginning and the ending, saith the Lord, which is, and which was, and which is to come, the Almighty*). You know the end from the beginning (**Isaiah 46:9-10** *Remember the former things of old: for I am God, and there is none else; I am God, and there is none like me, 10 Declaring the end from the beginning, and from ancient times the things that are not yet done, saying, My counsel shall stand, and I will do all my pleasure*).

There is no one above You. There is no one beside You. There is no one like You, Lord. You are the creator of life (**Genesis 1:1** *In the beginning God created the heaven and the earth*).

You are the sustainer of life (**Psalm 3:5** *I laid me down and slept; I awaked; for the Lord sustained me*). It's in You that I live and move and have my being (**Acts 17:28** *For in him we live, and move, and have our being; as certain also of your own poets have said, For we are also his offspring*).

I command my spirit to worship You, Almighty God (**Psalm 96:1-9** *O sing unto the Lord a new song: sing unto the Lord, all the earth. 2 Sing unto the Lord, bless his name; shew forth his salvation from day to day. 3 Declare his glory among the heathen,* *his wonders among all people. 4 For the Lord is great, and greatly to be praised: he is to be feared above all gods. 5 For all the gods of the nations are idols: but the Lord made the heavens. 6 Honour and majesty are before him: strength and beauty are in his sanctuary. 7 Give unto the Lord, O ye kindreds of the people, give unto the Lord glory and strength. 8 Give unto the Lord the glory due unto his name: bring an offering, and come into his courts. 9 O worship the Lord in the beauty of holiness: fear before him, all the earth).*

You are my bread of life (**John 6:48-51** *I am that bread of life. 49 Your fathers did eat manna in the wilderness, and are dead. 50 This is the bread which cometh down from heaven, that a man may eat thereof, and not die. 51 I am the living bread which came down from heaven: if any man eat of this bread, he shall live forever: and the bread that I will give is my flesh, which I will give for the life of the world).*

You are my well of living water (**John 4:10** *Jesus answered and said unto her, If thou knewest the gift of God, and who it is that saith to thee, Give me to drink; thou wouldest have asked of him, and he would have given thee living water;* **John 4:14** *But whosoever drinketh of the water that I shall give him shall never thirst; but the water that I shall give him shall be in him a well of water springing up into everlasting life).* Consume me, oh God, with Your presence. Holy Spirit, I welcome You. Dwell in me forever and help me. I want my life to be a praise unto You, Lord, so inhabit my praises (**Psalm 22:3** *But thou art holy, O thou that inhabitest the praises of Israel).*

Bless the Lord, oh my soul; and all that is within me, bless Your holy name (**Psalm 103:1**).

Glorify Yourself in my life, oh great God, and use me as You will to make Your name more famous in this earth.

I will be courageous and strong as a lion as I glorify Your name in this earth (**Acts 4:29**-31 *And now, Lord, behold their threatenings: and grant unto thy servants, that with all boldness they may speak thy word, 30 By stretching forth thine hand to heal; and that signs and wonders may be done by the name of thy holy child Jesus. 31 And when they had prayed, the place was shaken where they were assembled together; and they were all filled with the Holy Ghost, and they spake the word of God with boldness;* **Proverbs 28:1** *The wicked flee when no man pursueth: but the righteous are bold as a lion;* **Proverbs 30:30** *A lion which is strongest among beasts, and turneth not away for any).*

I won't just cope, and I won't just survive, but I will thrive. I will live life to the fullest and declare Your greatness until I breathe my last breath (**Psalm 118:**17 *I shall not die, but live, and declare the works of the Lord).*

All In God's Hands

My life is not my own (**1 Corinthians 6:19-20** *What? know ye not that your body is the temple of the Holy Ghost which is in you, which ye have of God, and ye are not your own? 20 For ye are bought with a price: therefore glorify God in your body, and in your spirit, which are God's*). Lord, I release all control and I give myself completely to You. Spirit of the living God, magnify Yourself in me and shine!!! You are my help, and my hope is in You (**Psalm 121:2** *My help cometh from the Lord, which made heaven and earth*; **Romans 15:4** *For whatsoever things were written aforetime were written for our learning, that we through patience and comfort of the scriptures might have hope*, **Romans 15:13** *Now the God of hope fill you with all joy and peace in believing, that ye may abound in hope, through the power of the Holy Ghost*).

I command myself to speak with and live in earnest expectation of Your will being done in my life and on this earth, as it is in heaven (**Matthew 6:10** *Thy kingdom come, Thy will be done in earth, as it is in heaven*).

I am who You say I am and I will be who You created me to be, Father, because You have called me, You are faithful, and You will cause it to be so (**1 Thessalonians 5:24** *Faithful is he that calleth you, who also will do it*).

You do all things well and nothing is too hard for You (**Jeremiah 32:17** *Ah Lord God! behold, thou hast made the heaven and the earth by thy great power and stretched out arm, and there is nothing too hard for thee*), so I trust You with my whole heart and I won't lean to my own understanding, but in all my ways I will acknowledge You, knowing that You will direct my path (**Proverbs 3:5-6** *Trust in the Lord with all thine heart; and lean not unto thine own understanding. 6 In all thy ways acknowledge him, and he shall direct thy paths*).

I exchange my wisdom, my understanding, and my knowledge for Yours because Yours is the best!!! (**Proverbs 3:7** *Be not wise in thine own eyes: fear the Lord, and depart from evil*; **James 3:17** *But the wisdom that is from above is first pure, then peaceable, gentle, and easy to be intreated, full of mercy and good fruits, without partiality, and without hypocrisy*).

I accept Your Holy Word, the Bible, to be entirely true (**2 Timothy 3:16** *All scripture is given by inspiration of God, and is profitable for doctrine, for reproof, for correction, for instruction in righteousness*).

In the Holy Bible, You promised to bless me and You cannot lie (**Romans 4:6-8** *Even as David also describeth the blessedness of the man, unto whom God imputeth righteousness without works, 7 Saying, Blessed are they whose iniquities are forgiven, and whose sins are covered. 8 Blessed is the man to whom the Lord will not impute sin;* **Numbers 23:19-20** *God is not a man, that he should lie; neither the son of man, that he should repent: hath he said, and shall he not do it? Or hath he spoken, and shall he not make it good? 20 Behold, I have received commandment to bless: and he hath blessed; and I cannot reverse it*). Therefore, I am disciplined to confess Your Word over my life, believe it, and put it into action. I refuse to stray from this practice because things that are impossible on my own, are possible with You (**Matthew**

19:26 *But Jesus beheld them, and said unto them, With men this is impossible; but with God all things are possible*), and if I can believe, all things are possible to them that believe (**Mark 9:23** *Jesus said unto him, If thou canst believe, all things are possible to him that believeth*).

I believe that You are the same God that manifested Your power and Your glory in the lives of the people in the Bible in times past, and You have no respect of persons, so now it's my turn (**Hebrews 13:8** *Jesus Christ the same yesterday, and to day, and for ever;* **John 14:21** *He that hath my commandments, and keepeth them, he it is that loveth me: and he that loveth me shall be loved of my Father, and I will love him, and will manifest myself to him;* **Romans 2:11** *For there is no respect of persons with God*).

I believe that You can do exceeding abundantly above all that I can ask or think according to the power that works in me, (**Ephesians 3:20** *Now unto him that is able to do exceeding abundantly above all that we ask or think, according to the power that worketh in us*), so <u>Dear Heavenly Father, all these things I ask</u> (**Matthew 7:11** *If ye then, being evil, know how to give good gifts unto your children, how much more shall your Father which is in heaven give good things to them that ask him*), <u>I think</u> (**Proverbs 23:7** *For as he thinketh in his heart, so is he*), <u>I pray</u> (**Mark 11:24** *Therefore I say unto you, What things soever ye desire, when ye pray, believe that ye receive them, and ye shall have them;* **John 15:**7 *If ye abide in me, and my words abide in you, ye shall ask what ye will, and it shall be done unto you*), and <u>I decree</u> to be so (**Job 22:**28 *Thou shalt also decree a thing, and it shall be established unto thee: and the light shall shine upon thy ways*), <u>by faith</u> (**Hebrews 11:6** *But without faith it is impossible to please him: for he that cometh to God must believe that he is, and that he is a rewarder of them that diligently seek him;* **Hebrews10:23** *Let us hold fast the profession of our faith without wavering; (for* *he is faithful that promised*), <u>according to Your Word</u> (**Isaiah 55:9-11** *For as the heavens are higher than the earth, so are my ways higher than your ways, and my thoughts than your thoughts. 10 For as the rain cometh down, and the snow from heaven, and returneth not thither, but watereth the earth, and maketh it bring forth and bud, that it may give seed to the sower, and bread to the eater: 11 So shall my word be that goeth forth out of my mouth: it shall not return unto me void, but it shall accomplish that which I please, and it shall prosper in the thing whereto I sent it;* **Mark 13:31** *Heaven and earth shall pass away: but my words shall not pass away*), and <u>in the matchless name of Jesus</u> (**Philippians 2:9** *Wherefore God also hath highly exalted him, and given him a name which is above every name*).

NOW UNTO HIM WHO IS ABLE TO KEEP ME FROM FALLING AND TO PRESENT ME FAULTLESS BEFORE THE PRESENCE OF HIS GLORY WITH EXCEEDING JOY, TO THE ONLY WISE GOD MY SAVIOR, BE GLORY AND MAJESTY, DOMINION AND POWER, BOTH NOW AND FOREVER. AMEN (**Jude 24-25**).

My Prayer List

Date of Prayer	Request	Scripture Promise	Date Answered

Notes

_____

_____

_____

_____

_____

_____

_____

_____

_____

_____

_____

_____

_____

_____

_____

_____

_____

My Prayer List

Date of Prayer	Request	Scripture Promise	Date Answered

Notes

Notes

Notes

_____

_____

_____

_____

_____

_____

_____

_____

_____

_____

_____

_____

_____

_____

_____

_____

_____

_____

_____

_____

Notes

_____

_____

_____

_____

_____

_____

_____

_____

_____

_____

_____

_____

_____

_____

_____

_____

_____

_____

Notes

_____

_____

_____

_____

_____

_____

_____

_____

_____

_____

_____

_____

_____

_____

_____

_____

_____

_____

_____

About Tina Campbell

Known to much of the world as one half of the gospel duo Mary Mary, Tina Campbell is an accomplished and multi-award winning singer and songwriter. She has already achieved a lifetime of success having won 4 Grammy Awards, American Music Awards, NAACP Image Awards, Soul Train Awards, Stellar Awards, Dove Awards, and the ASCAP's acclaimed Golden Note Award. Her additional accomplishments include having sold 5 million records and counting, and establishing herself as a contender in TV land through several seasons of her hit reality show, "The Mary Mary Show." Tina's career in music and television alongside her sister, Erica Campbell, the other half of Mary Mary, has spanned more than a decade.

She has now moved to the forefront to share this new book, a new solo album entitled "IT'S PERSONAL," and a one woman stage presentation entitled "AN EVENING WITH TINA CAMPBELL," which is a dramatic exploration of the journey of how the most dreadful test of her life became the most beautiful testimony.

The singer/songwriter/TV star and author has relied on her faith through some of life's most overwhelming challenges and, because of her faith, was able to overcome them. In light of this, sharing that faith with the world through singing, writing, and speaking has become her greatest passion.

Tina Campbell is also the proud wife of Teddy Campbell and the proud mother of 5 children. She says, "Of all that my life has consisted of, my greatest accomplishment is my healthy happy family that prays together and stays together through it all."

More Resources by Tina Campbell

Music album:

Contact Information

Publisher: Gee Tree Creative
21700 Oxnard Street, Suite 2030
Woodland Hills, CA 91367
www.IamTinaCampbell.com